FAR OFF

OR,

Asia and Australia Described

FAR OFF;

OR,

Asia and Australia Described

WITH

ANECDOTES AND ILLUSTRATIONS

FAVELL LEE MORTIMER

GYAN

Published by

GYAN

Gyan Publishing House
5, Ansari Road
Darayaganj, New Delhi-110002
Phone: 011-47034999, 9811692060
E-mail: books@gyanbooks.com

Distribution Network
gyanbooks.com
India, USA, Canada, UK, Australia, France

ISBN : 978-81-212-9616-8 (PB)
First Published, 1854

2nd Impression 2023

Printed at: Gyan Press, Delhi.

FAR OFF OR ASIA AND AUSTRALIA DESCRIBED
Author: FAVELL LEE MORTIMER

"O Ma'am, that's sweet! Jesus Christ is OUR Redeemer." p. 3.

R. CARTER & BROTHERS New York.

FAR OFF;

OR,

Asia and Australia Described.

WITH

ANECDOTES AND ILLUSTRATIONS.

BY THE
AUTHOR OF "THE PEEP OF DAY
ETC. ETC. ETC.

1854.

In the Frontispiece may be seen an English lady, who went to live upon Mount Sion to teach little Jewesses and little Mahomedans to know the Saviour. That lady has led three of her young scholars to a plain just beyond the gates of Jerusalem; and while two of them are playing together, she is listening to little Esther, a Jewess of eight years old. The child is fond of sitting by her friend, and of hearing about the Son of David. She has just been singing,

> "Glory, honor, praise, and power,
> Be unto the Lamb forever,
> Jesus Christ is our Redeemer,
> Hallelujah, praise the Lord;"

and now she is saying, "O, ma'am, that's sweet! Jesus Christ is *our* Redeemer, *our* Redeemer: no *man* can redeem his brother, no *money*,—nothing—but only the precious blood of Christ."

Preface.

This little work pleads for the notice of parents and teachers on the same grounds as its predecessor, "Near Home."

Its plea is not completeness, nor comprehensiveness, nor depth of research, nor splendor of description; but the very reverse,—its simple, superficial, desultory character, as better adapted to the volatile beings for whom it is designed.

Too long have their immortal minds been captivated by the adventures and achievements of knights and princesses, of fairies and magicians; it is time to excite their interest in real persons, and real events. In childhood that taste is formed which leads the youth to delight in novels, and romances; a taste which has become so general, that every town has its circulating library, and every shelf in that library is filled with works of fiction.

While these fascinating inventions are in course of perusal, many a Bible is unopened, or if opened, hastily skimmed; many a seat in church is unoccupied, or if occupied, the service, and the sermon disregarded—so intense is the sympathy of the novel reader with his hero, or his heroine.

And what is the effect of the perusal? Many a young mind, inflated with a desire for admiration and adventure, grows tired of home, impatient of restraint, indifferent to simple pleasures, and averse to sacred instructions. How important, therefore, early to endeavor to prevent a taste for FICTION, by cherishing a taste for FACTS.

But this is not the only aim of the present work; it seeks also to excite an interest in *those* facts which ought *most* to interest immortal beings—facts relative to souls, and their eternal happiness—to God, and his infinite glory.

These are the facts which engage the attention of the inhabitants of heaven. We know not whether the births of princes, and the coronations of monarchs are noticed by the angelic hosts; but we do know that the repentance of a sinner, be he Hindoo or Hottentot, is celebrated by their melodious voices in rapturous symphonies.

Therefore "Far Off" desires to interest its little readers in the labors of missionaries,—men despised and maligned by the world, but honored and beloved by the Saviour of the world. An account of the scenery and natives of various countries, is calculated to prepare the young mind for reading with intelligence those little Missionary Magazines, which appear every month, written in so attractive a style, and adorned with such beautiful illustrations. Parents have no longer reason to complain of the difficulty of finding sacred entertainment for their children on Sunday, for these pleasing messengers,—if carefully dealt out,—one or two on each Sabbath, would afford a never failing supply.

To form great and good characters, the mind must be trained to delight in TRUTH,—not in comic rhymes, in sentimental tales, and skeptical poetry. The truth revealed in God's Holy Word, should constitute the firm basis of education; and the works of Creation and Providence the superstructure while the Divine blessing can alone rear and cement the edifice.

Parents, train up your children to serve God, and to enjoy his presence forever; and if there be amongst them—an EXTRAORDINARY child, train him up with extraordinary care, lest instead of doing extraordinary *good* he should do extraordinary *evil*, and be plunged into extraordinary misery.

Train up—the child of imagination—not to dazzle, like Byron, but to enlighten, like Cowper: the child of wit—not to create profane mirth, like Voltaire, but to promote holy joy, like Bunyan: the child of reflection—not to weave dangerous sophistries, like Hume, but to wield powerful arguments, like Chalmers: the child of sagacity—not to gain advantages for himself, like Cromwell, but for his country, like Washington: the child of eloquence—not to astonish the multitude, like Sheridan, but to plead for the miserable, like Wilberforce: the child of ardor—not to be the herald of delusions, like Swedenbourg, but to be the champion of truth, like Luther: the child of enterprise—not to devastate a Continent, like the conquering Napoleon, but to scatter blessings over an Ocean, like the missionary Williams:—and, if the child be a prince,—train him up—not to reign in pomp and pride like the fourteenth Louis, but to rule in the fear of God, like our own great ALFRED.

Contents.

FAR OFF.

Asia.

Of the four quarters of the world—Asia is the most glorious.

There the first man lived.

There the Son of God lived.

There the apostles lived.

There the Bible was written.

Yet now there are very few Christians in Asia: though there are more people there than in any other quarter of the globe.

The Holy Land.

Of all the countries in the world which would you rather see?

Would it not be the land where Jesus lived?

He was the Son of God: He loved us and died for us.

What is the land called where He lived? Canaan was once its name: but now Palestine, or the Holy Land.

Who lives there now?

Alas! alas! The Jews who once lived there are cast out of it. There are some Jews there; but the Turks are the lords over the land. You know the Turks believe in Mahomet.

What place in the Holy Land do you wish most to visit?

Some childrem will reply, Bethlehem, because Jesus was born there; another will answer, Nazareth, because Jesus was brought up there; and another will say, "Jerusalem," because He died there.

I will take you first to

BETHLEHEM.

A good minister visited this place, accompanied by a train of servants, and camels, and asses.

It is not easy to travel in Palestine, for wheels are never seen there, because the paths are too steep, and rough, and narrow for carriages.

Bethlehem is on a steep hill, and a white road of chalk leads up to the gate. The traveller found the streets narrow, dark, and dirty. He lodged in a convent, kept by Spanish monks. He was shown into a large room with carpets and cushions on the floor. There he was to sleep. He was led up to the roof of the house to see the prospect. He looked, and beheld the fields below where the shepherds once watched their flocks by night: and far off he saw the rocky mountains where David once hid himself from Saul.

But the monks soon showed him a more curious sight. They took him into their church, and then down some narrow stone steps into a round room beneath. "Here," said they, "Jesus was born." The floor was of white marble, and silver lamps were burning in it. In one corner, close to the wall, was a marble trough, lined with blue satin. "There," said the monks, "is the manger where Jesus was laid." "Ah!" thought the traveller, "it was not in such a manger that my Saviour rested his infant head; but in a far meaner place."

These monks have an image of a baby, which they call Jesus. On Christmas-day they dress it in swaddling-clothes and lay it in the manger: and then fall down and worship it.

The next day, as the traveller was ready to mount his camel, the people of Bethlehem came with little articles which they had made. But he would not buy them, because they were images of the Virgin Mary and her holy child, and little white crosses of mother-of-pearl. They were very pretty: but they were idols, and God hates idols.

JERUSALEM.

Here our Lord was crucified.

Is there any child who does not wish to hear about it?

The children of Jerusalem once loved the Lord, and sang his praises in the temple. Their young voices pleased their Saviour, though not half so sweet as angels' songs.

Which is the place where the temple stood?

It is Mount Moriah. There is a splendid building there now.

Is it the temple? O no, that was burned many hundreds of years ago. It is the Mosque of Omar that you see; it is the most magnificent mosque in all the world. How sad to think that Mahomedans should worship now in the very spot where once the

Son of God taught the people. No Jew, no Christian may go into that mosque. The Turks stand near the gate to keep off both Jews and Christians.

Every Friday evening a very touching scene takes place near this mosque. There are some large old stones there, and the Jews say they are part of their old temple wall: so they come at the beginning of their Sabbath (which is on Friday evening) and sit in a row opposite the stones. There they read their Hebrew Old Testaments, then kneel low in the dust, and repeat their prayers with their mouths close to the old stones: because they think that all prayers whispered between the cracks and crevices of these stones will be heard by God. Some Jewesses come, wrapped from head to foot in long white veils, and they gently moan and softly sigh over Jerusalem in ruins.

What Jesus said has come to pass, "Behold, your house is left unto you desolate." The thought of this sad day made Jesus weep, and now the sight of it makes the Jews weep.

But there is a place still dearer to our hearts than Mount Moriah. It is Calvary. There is a church there: but such a church! a church full of images and crosses. Roman Catholics worship there—and Greeks too: and they often fight in it, for they hate one another, and have fierce quarrels.

That church is called "The Church of the Holy Sepulchre." It is pretended that Christ's tomb or sepulchre is in it. Turks stand at the door and make Christians pay money before they will let them in.

When they enter, what do they see?

In one corner a stone seat. "There," say the monks, "Jesus sat when He was crowned with thorns." In another part there is a stone pillar. "There," say the monks, "He was scourged." There is a high place in the middle of the church with stairs leading up to it. When you stand there the monks say, "This is the top of Calvary, where the cross stood." But we know that the monks do not speak the truth, for the Romans destroyed Jerusalem soon after Christ's crucifixion, and no one knows the very place where He suffered.

On Good Friday the monks carry all round the church an image of the Saviour as large as life, and they fasten it upon a cross, and take it down again, and put it in the sepulchre, and they take it out again on Easter Sunday. How foolish and how wrong are these customs! It was not in this way the apostles showed their love to Christ, but by preaching his word.

Mount Zion is the place where David brought the ark with songs and music. There is a church where the Gospel is preached and prayers are offered up in Hebrew, (the Jew's language.) The minister is called the Bishop of Jerusalem. He is a Protestant. A few Jews come to the church at Mount Zion, and some have believed in the Lord Jesus.

And there is a school there where little Jews and Jewesses and little Mahomedans sit side by side, while a Christian lady teaches them about Jesus. In the evening, after school, she takes them out to play on the green grass near the city. A little Jewess once much pleased this kind teacher as she was sitting on a stone looking at the children playing. Little Esther repeated the verse—

Glory, honor, praise and power
Be unto the Lamb forever;
Jesus Christ is our Redeemer,
Hallelujah, praise the Lord!

and then she said very earnestly, "O, ma'am, how sweet to think that Jesus is *our* Redeemer. No *man* can redeem his brother: no money—no money can do it—only the precious blood of Jesus Christ." Little Esther seemed as if she loved Jesus, as those children did who sang his praises in the temple so many years ago.

But there is another place—very sad, but very sweet—where you must come. Go down that valley

—cross that small stream—(there is a narrow bridge) —see those low stone walls—enter: it is the Garden of Gethsemane. Eight aged olive-trees are still standing there; but Jesus comes there no more with his beloved disciples. What a night was that when He wept and prayed—when the angel comforted Him—and Judas betrayed Him.

The mountain just above Gethsemane is the Mount of Olives. Beautiful olive-trees are growing there still. There is a winding path leading to the top. The Saviour trod upon that Mount just before he was caught up into heaven. His feet shall stand there again, and every eye shall see the Saviour in his glory. But will every eye be glad to see Him?

O no; there will be bitter tears then flowing from many eyes.

And what kind of a city is Jerusalem?

It is a sad and silent city. The houses are dark and dirty, the streets are narrow, and the pavement rough. There are a great many very old Jews there. Jews come from all countries when they are old to Jerusalem, that they may die and be buried there. Their reason is that they think that all Jews who are buried in their burial-ground at Jerusalem will be raised *first* at the last day, and will be happy forever. Most of the old Jews are very poor: though money is sent to them every year from the Jews in Europe.

There are also a great many sick Jews in Jerusalem, because it is such an unhealthy place. The water in the wells and pools gets very bad in summer, and gives the ague and even the plague. Good English Christians have sent a doctor to Jerusalem to cure the poor sick people. One little girl of eleven years old came among the rest—all in rags and with bare feet: she was an orphan, and she lived with a Jewish washerwoman. The doctor went to see the child in her home. Where was it? It was near the mosque, and the way to it was down a narrow, dark passage, leading to a small close yard. The old woman lived in one room with her grandchildren and the orphan: there was a divan at each end, that is, the floor was raised for people to sleep on. The orphan was not allowed to sleep on the divans, but she had a heap of rags for her bed in another part. The child's eyes glistened with delight at the sight of her kind friend the doctor. He asked her whether she went to school. This question made the whole family laugh: for no one in Jerusalem teaches girls to read except the kind Christian lady I told you of.

THE DEAD SEA.

THE most gloomy and horrible place in the Holy Land is the Dead Sea. In that place there once stood four wicked cities, and God destroyed them with fire and brimstone.

You have heard of Sodom and Gomorrah.

A clergyman who went to visit the Dead Sea rode on horseback, and was accompanied by men to guard him on the way, as there are robbers hid among the rocks. He took some of the water of the Dead Sea in his mouth, that he might taste it, and he found it salt and bitter; but he would not swallow it, nor would he bathe in it.

He went next to look at the River Jordan. How different a place from the dreary, desolate Dead Sea! Beautiful trees grow on the banks, and the ends of the branches dip into the stream. The minister chose a part quite covered with branches and bathed there, and as the waters went over his head, he thought, "My Saviour was baptized in this river." But he did not think, as many pilgrims do who come here every year, that his sins were washed away by the water: no, he well knew that Christ's blood alone cleanses from sin. There is a place where the Roman Catholics bathe, and another where the Greeks bathe every year; they would not on any account bathe in the same part, because they disagree so much.

After drinking some of the sweet soft water of Jordan, the minister travelled from Jericho to Jerusalem. He went the very same way that the good Samaritan travelled who once found a poor Jew lying half-killed by thieves. Even to this day thieves often attack travellers in these parts: because the way is so lonely, and so rugged, and so full of places where thieves can hide themselves.

A horse must be a very good climber to carry a traveller along the steep, rough, and narrow paths, and a traveller must be a bold man to venture to go to the edge of the precipices, and near the robbers' caves.

SAMARIA.

In the midst of Palestine is the well where the Lord spoke so kindly to the woman of Samaria. In the midst of a beautiful valley there is a heap of rough stones: underneath is the well. But it is not easy to drink water out of this well. For the stone on the top is so heavy, that it requires many people to remove it: and then the well is deep, and a very long rope is necessary to reach the water. The clergyman (of whom I have spoken so often) had nothing to draw with ; therefore, even if he could have removed the stone, he could not have drunk of the water. The water must be very cool and refreshing, because it lies so far away from the heat. That was the reason the Samaritan woman came so far to draw it : for there were other streams nearer the city, but there was no water like the water of Jacob's well.

The city where that woman lived was called Sychar. It is still to be seen, and it is still full of people. You remember that the men of that city listened to the words of Jesus, and perhaps that is the reason it has not been destroyed. The country around is the most fruitful in all Canaan ; there are such gardens of melons and cucumbers, and such groves of mulberry-trees.

GALILEE.

How different from Sychar is Capernaum ! That was the city where Jesus lived for a long while, where he preached and did miracles. It was on the borders of the lake of Genesareth. The traveller inquired of the people near the lake, where Capernaum once stood ; but no one knew of such a place : it is utterly destroyed. Jesus once said, "Woe unto Capernaum." Why? Because it repented not.

The lake of Genesareth looked smooth as glass when the traveller saw it; but he heard that dreadful storms sometimes ruffled those smooth waters. It was a sweet and lovely spot; not gloomy and horrible like the Dead Sea. The shepherds were there leading their flocks among the green hills where once the multitude sat down while Jesus fed them.

Not very far off is the city where Jesus lived when he was a boy.

NAZARETH.—All around are rugged rocky hills. In old times it was considered a wicked city; perhaps it got this bad name from wicked people coming here to hide themselves: and it seems just fit for a hiding-place. From the top of one of the high crags the Nazarenes once attempted to hurl the blessed Saviour.

There is a Roman Catholic convent there, where the minister lodged. He was much disturbed all day by the noise in the town; not the noise of carts and wagons, for there are none in Canaan, but of screaming children, braying asses, and grunting camels. One of his servants came to him complaining that he had lost his purse with all his wages. He had left it in his cell, and when he came back it was gone. Who could have taken it? It was clear one of the servants of the convent must have stolen it, for one of them had the key of the room. The travellers went to the judge of the town to complain; but the judge, who was a Turk, was asleep, and no one was allowed to awake him. In the evening, when he did awake, he would not see justice done, because he said he had nothing to do with the servants at the convent, as they were Christians. Nazareth, you see, is still a wicked city, where robbery is committed and not punished.

There is much to make the traveller sad as he wanders about the Holy Land.

That land was once *fruitful*, but now it is barren. It is not surprising that no one plants and sows in the fields, because the Turks would take away the harvests.

Once it was a *peaceful* land, but now there are so many enemies that every man carries a gun to defend himself.

Once it was a *holy* land, but now Mahomet is honored, and not the God of Israel.

When shall it again be fruitful, and peaceful, and holy? When the Jews shall repent of their sins and turn to the Lord. Then, says the prophet Ezekiel, (xxxvi. 35,) "They shall say, This land that was desolate is become like the garden of Eden."*

* Taken chiefly from "A Pastor's Memorial," by the Rev. George Fisk.

Syria.

THOSE who love the Holy Land will like to hear about Syria also; for Abraham lived there before he came into Canaan. Therefore the Israelites were taught to say when they offered a basket of fruit to God, "A Syrian was my father." It was a heathen land in old times; and it is now a Mahomedan land; though there are a few Christians there, but very ignorant Christians, who know nothing of the Bible.

Syria is a beautiful land, and famous for its grand mountains, called Lebanon. The same clergyman who travelled through the Holy Land went to Lebanon also. He had to climb up very steep places on horseback, and slide down some, as slanting as the roof of a house. But the Syrian horses are very sure-footed. It is the custom for the colts from a month old to follow their mothers; and so when a rider mounts the back of the colt's mother, the young creature follows, and it learns to scramble up steep places, and to slide down; even through the towns the colt trots after its mother, and soon becomes accustomed to all kinds of sights and sounds: so that Syrian horses neither shy nor stumble.

The traveller was much surprised at the dress of the women of Lebanon: for on their heads they wear silver horns sticking out from under their veils, the strangest head-dress that can be imagined.

There are sweet flowers growing on the sides of Lebanon; but at the top there are ice and snow.

The traveller ate some ice, and gave some to the horses; and the poor beasts devoured it eagerly, and seemed quite refreshed by their cold meal.

The snow of Lebanon is spoken of in the Bible as very pure and refreshing. "Will a man leave the snow of Lebanon, which cometh from the rock of the field?"—Jer. xviii. 14.

The traveller earnestly desired to behold the cedars of Lebanon: for a great deal is said about them in the Bible; indeed, the temple of Solomon was built of those cedars. It was not easy to get close to them; for there were craggy rocks all around: but at last the traveller reached them, and stood beneath their shade. There were twelve very large old trees, and their boughs met at the top, and kept off the heat of the sun. These trees might be compared to holy men, grown old in the service of God: for this is God's

A CEDAR TREE.

p. 32

promise to his servants,—"The righteous shall flourish like the palm-tree: he shall grow like a cedar in Lebanon."—Psalm xc. 11, 12.

DAMASCUS.

This is the capital of Syria.

It is perhaps the most ancient city in the world. Even in the time of Abraham, Damascus was a city; for his servant Eliezer came from it.

But Damascus is most famous, on account of a great event which once happened near it. A man going towards that city suddenly saw in the heavens a light brighter than the sun, and heard a voice from on high, calling him by his name. Beautiful as the city was, he saw not its beauty as he entered it, for he had been struck blind by the great light. That man was the great apostle Paul.

Who can help thinking of him among the gardens of fruit-trees surrounding Damascus?

The damask rose is one of the beauties of Damascus. There is one spot quite covered with this lovely red rose.

I will now give an account of a visit a stranger paid to a rich man in Damascus. He went through dull and narrow streets, with no windows looking into the streets. He stopped before a low door, and was shown into a large court behind the house. There was a fountain in the midst of the court, and flower-pots all round. The visitor was then led into a room with a marble floor, but with no furniture except scarlet cushions. To refresh him after his journey, he was taken to the bath. There a man covered him with a lather of soap and water, then dished a quantity of hot water over him, and then rubbed him till he was quite dry and warm.

When he came out of the bath, two servants brought him some sherbet. It is a cooling drink made of lemon-juice and grape-juice mixed with water.

The master of the house received the stranger very politely: he not only shook hands with him, but afterwards he kissed his own hand, as a mark of respect to his guest. The servants often kissed the visitor's hand.

The dinner lasted a long while, for only one dish was brought up at a time. Of course there were no ladies at the dinner, for in Mahomedan countries they are always hidden. There were two lads there, who were nephews to the master of the house; and the visitor was much surprised to observe that they did not sit down to dinner with the company; but that they stood near their uncle, directing the servants what to bring him; and now and then presenting a cup of wine to him, or his guests. But it is the custom in Syria for young people to wait upon their elders; however, they may speak to the company while they are waiting upon them.

Damascus used to be famous for its swords: but now the principal things made there, are stuffs embroidered with silver, and boxes of curious woods, as well as red and yellow slippers. The Syrians always wear yellow slippers, and when they walk out they put on red slippers over the yellow. If you want to buy any of the curious works of Damascus, you must go to the bazaars in the middle of the town; there the sellers sit as in a market-place, and display their goods.

SCHOOLS.—It is not the custom in Syria for girls to learn to read. But a few years ago, a good Syrian, named Assaad, opened a school for little girls as well as for boys.

It was easy to get the little boys to come; but the mothers did not like to send their little girls. They laughed, and said, "Who ever heard of a girl going to school? Girls need not learn to read." The first girl who attended Assaad's school was named Angoul, which means "Angel." Where is the child that deserves such a name? Nowhere; for there is none righteous, no, not one. Angoul belonged not to Mahomedan parents, but to those called Christians; yet the Christians in Syria are almost as ignorant as heathens.

Angoul had been taught to spin silk; for her father had a garden of mulberry-trees, and a quantity of silk worms. She was of so much use in spinning, that her mother did not like to spare her: but the little maid promised, that if she might go to school, she would spin faster than ever when she came home. How happy she was when she obtained leave to go! See her when the sun has just risen, about six o'clock, tripping to school. She is twelve years old. Her eyes are dark, but her hair is light. Angoul has not been scorched by the sun, like many Syrian girls, because she has sat in-doors at her wheel during the heat of the day. She is dressed in a loose red gown, and a scarlet cap with a yellow handkerchief twisted round it like a turban.

At school Angoul is very attentive, both while she is reading in her Testament, and while she is writing on her tin slate with a reed dipped in ink. She returns home at noon through the burning sun, and comes to school again to stay till five. Then it is cool and pleasant, and Angoul spins by her mother's side in the lovely garden of fruit-trees before the house. Has she not learned to sing many a sweet verse about the garden above, and the heavenly husbandman? As she watches the budding vine, she can think now of Him who said, "I am the true vine." As she sits beneath the olive-tree, she can call to mind the words, "I am like a green olive-tree in the house of my God." Angoul is growing like an angel, if she takes delight in meditating on the word of God.*

* Extracted chiefly from the Rev. George Fisk's "Pastor's Memorial," and Kinnear's Travels.

Arabia.

This is the land in which the Israelites wandered for forty years. You have heard what a dry, dreary, desert place the wilderness was. There is still a wilderness in Arabia; and there are still wanderers in it; not Israelites, but Arabs. These men live in tents, and go from place to place with their large flocks of sheep and goats. But there are other Arabs who live in towns, as we do.

Do you know who is the father of the Arabs?

The same man who is the father of the Jews.

What, was Abraham their father?

Yes, he was.

Do you remember Abraham's ungodly son, Ishmael?

He was cast out of his father's house for mocking his little brother Isaac, and he went into Arabia.

And what sort of people are the Arabs?

Wild and fierce people.

Travellers are afraid of passing through Arabia, lest

the Arabs should rob and murder them; and no one has ever been able to conquer the Arabs. The Arabs are very proud, and will not bear the least affront. Sometimes one man says to another, "The wrong side of your turban is out." This speech is considered an affront never to be forgotten. The Arabs are so unforgiving and revengeful that they will seek to kill a man year after year. One man was observed to carry about a small dagger. He said his reason was, he was hoping some day to meet his enemy and kill him.

Of what religion are this revengeful people? The Mahomedan.

Mahomed was an Arab. It is thought a great honor to be descended from him. Those men who say Mahomed is their father wear a green turban, and very proud they are of their green turbans, even though they may only be beggars.

The Arabian Women.—They are shut up like the women in Syria when they live in towns, but the women in tents are obliged to walk about; therefore they wear a thick veil over their face, with small holes for their eyes to peep out.

The poor women wear a long shirt of white or blue; but the rich women wrap themselves in magnificent shawls. To make themselves handsome, they blacken their eyelids, paint their nails red, and wear gold rings in their ears and noses. They delight in fine furniture. A room lined with looking-glasses, and with a ceiling of looking-glasses, is thought charming.

ARAB TENTS.—They are black, being made of the hair of black goats. Some of them are so large that they are divided into three rooms, one for the cattle, one for the men, and one for the women.

ARAB CUSTOMS.—The Arabs sit on the ground, resting on their heels, and for tables they have low stools. A large dish of rice and minced mutton is placed on the table, and immediately every hand is thrust into it; and in a moment it is empty. Then another dish is brought, and another; and sometimes fourteen dishes of rice, one after the other, till all the company are satisfied. They eat very fast, and each retires from dinner as soon as he likes, without waiting for the rest. After dinner they drink water, and a small cup of coffee without milk or sugar. Then they smoke for many hours.

The Arabs do not indulge in eating or drinking too much, and this is one of the best parts of their character.

THE THREE EVILS OF ARABIA.

The first evil is want of water. There is no river in Arabia: and the small streams are often dried up by the heat.

The second evil is many locusts, which come in countless swarms, and devour every green thing.

The third evil is the burning winds. When a traveller feels it coming, he throws himself on the ground, covering his face with his cloak, lest the hot sand should be blown up his nostrils. Sometimes men and horses are choked by this sand.

These are the three great evils; but there is a still greater, the religion of Mahomed: for this injures the soul; the other evils only hurt the body.

THE THREE ANIMALS OF ARABIA.

The animals for which Arabia is famous are animals to ride upon.

Two of them are often seen in England; though here they are not nearly as fine as in Arabia; but the third animal is never used in England. Most English boys have ridden upon an ass. In Arabia the ass is a handsome and spirited creature. The horse is strong and swift, and yet obedient and gentle. The camel is just suited to Arabia. His feet are fit to tread upon the burning sands; because the soles are more like India-rubber than like flesh: his hard mouth, lined with horn, is not hurt by the prickly plants of the desert; and his hump full of fat is as good to him as a bag of provisions: for on a journey the fat helps to support him, and enables him to do with very little food. Besides all this, his inside is so made that he can live without water for three days.

A dromedary is a swifter kind of camel, and is just as superior to a camel as a riding-horse is to a cart-horse.

THE THREE PRODUCTIONS OF ARABIA.

These are coffee, dates, and gums.

For these Arabia is famous.

The coffee plants are shrubs. The hills are covered with them; the white blossoms look beautiful among the dark green leaves, and so do the red berries.

The dates grow on the palm-trees; and they are the chief food of the Arabs. The Arabs despise those countries where there are no dates.

There are various sweet-smelling gums that flow from Arabian trees.

THE THREE PARTS OF ARABIA.

You see from what I have just said that there are plants and trees in Arabia. Then it is clear that the whole land is not a desert. No, it is not; there is only a part called Desert Arabia; that is on the north. There is a part in the middle almost as bad, called Stony Arabia, yet some sweet plants grow there; but there is a part in the south called Happy Arabia, where grow abundance of fragrant spices, and of well-flavored coffee.

THE THREE CITIES OF ARABIA.

Arabia has long been famous for three cities, called Mecca, Medina, and Mocha.

Mecca is considered the holiest city in the world. And why? Because the false prophet Mahomed was born there. On that account Mahomedans come from all parts of the world to worship in the great temple there. Sometimes Mecca is as full of people as a hive is full of bees.

Of all the cities in the East, Mecca is the gayest, because the houses have windows looking into the streets. In these houses are lodgings for the pilgrims.

And what is it the pilgrims worship?

A great black stone, which they say the angel Gabriel brought down from heaven as a foundation for Mahomed's house. They kiss it seven times, and after each kiss they walk round it.

Then they bathe in a well, which they say is the well the angel showed to Hagar in the desert, and they think the waters of this well can wash away all their sins. Alas! they know not of the blood which can wash away *all* sin.

Medina contains the tomb of Mahomed; yet it is not thought so much of as Mecca. Perhaps the Mahomedans do not like to be reminded that Mahomed died like any other man, and never rose again.

Mocha.—This is a part whence very fine coffee is sent to Europe.

TRAVELS IN THE DESERT.

Of all places in Arabia, which would you desire most to see? Would it not be Mount Sinai? Our great and glorious God once spoke from the top of that mountain.

I will tell you of an English clergyman who travelled to see that mountain. As he knew there were many robbers on the way, he hired an Arab sheikh to take care of him. A sheikh is a chief, or captain. Suleiman was a fine-looking man, dressed in a red shirt, with a shawl twisted round his waist, a purple cloak, and a red cap. His feet and legs were bare. His eyes were bright, his skin was brown, and his beard black. To his girdle were fastened a huge knife and pistols, and by his side hung a sword. This man brought a band of Arabs with him to defend the travellers from the robbers in the desert.

One day the whole party set out mounted on camels. After going some distance, a number of children were seen scampering among the rocks, and looking like brown monkeys. These were the children of the Arabs who accompanied the Englishman. The wild little creatures ran to their fathers, and saluted them in the respectful manner that Arab children are taught to do.

At last a herd of goats was seen with a fine boy of twelve years old leading them. He was the son of Suleiman. The father seemed to take great delight in this boy, and introduced him to the traveller. The kind gentleman riding on a camel, put down his hand to the boy. The little fellow, after touching the traveller's hand, kissed his own, according to the Arabian manner.

The way to Mount Sinai was very rough; indeed, the traveller was sometimes obliged to get off his camel, and to climb among the crags on hands and knees. How glad he was when the Arabs pointed to a mountain, and said, "That is Mount Sinai." With what fear and reverence he gazed upon it! Here it was that the voice of the great God was once heard speaking out of the midst of the smoke, and clouds, and darkness!

How strange it must be to see in this lonely gloomy spot, a great building! Yet there is one at the foot of the mountain. What can it be? A convent. See those high walls around. It is necessary to have high walls, because all around are bands of fierce robbers. It is even unsafe to have a door near the ground. There is a door quite high up in the wall; but what use can it be of, when there are no steps by which to reach it? Can you guess how people get in by this door? A rope is let down from the door to draw the people up. One by one they are drawn up. In the inside of the walls there are steps by which travellers go down into the convent below. The monks who live there belong to the Greek church.

The clergyman was lodged in a small cell spread with carpets and cushions, and he was waited upon by the monks.

These monks think that they lead a very holy life in the desert. They eat no meat, and they rise in the night to pray in their chapel. But God does not care for such service as this. He never commanded men to shut themselves up in a desert, but rather to do good in the world.

One day the monks told the traveller they would show him the place where the burning bush once stood. How could they know the place? However, they pretended to know it. They led the way to the chapel, then taking off their shoes, they went down some stone steps till they came to a round room under ground, with three lamps burning in the midst. "There," said the monks, "is the very spot where the burning bush once stood."

There were two things the traveller enjoyed while in the convent, the beautiful garden full of thick trees and sweet flowers; and the cool pure water from the well. Such water and such a garden in the midst of a desert were sweet indeed.

The Arabs, who accompanied the traveller, enjoyed much the plentiful meals provided at the convent; for the monks bought sheep from the shepherds around, to feed their guests. After leaving the convent, Suleiman was taken ill in consequence of having eaten too much while there. The clergyman gave him medicine, which cured him. The Arabs were very fond of their chief, and were so grateful to the stranger for giving him medicine, that they called him "the good physician." Suleiman himself showed his gratitude by bringing his own black coffee-pot into the tent of the stranger, and asking him to drink coffee with him; for such is the pride of an Arab chief, that he thinks it is a very great honor indeed for a stranger to share his meal.

But the traveller soon found that it is dangerous to pass through a desert. Why? Not on account of wild beasts, but of wild men. There was a tribe of Arabs very angry with Suleiman, because he was conducting the travellers through *their* part of the desert. They wanted to be the guides through that part, in hopes of getting rewarded by a good sum of money. You see how covetous they were. The love of money is the root of all evil.

These angry Arabs were hidden among the rocks and hills; and every now and then they came suddenly out of their hiding-places, and with a loud voice threatened to punish Suleiman.

How much alarmed the travellers were! but none more than Suleiman himself. He requested the clergyman to travel during the whole night, in order the sooner to get out of the reach of the enemy. The clergyman promised to go as far as he was able. What a journey it was! No one durst speak aloud to his companions, lest the enemies should be hidden among the rocks close by, and should overhear them. At midnight the whole company pitched their tents by the coast of the Red Sea. Early in the morning the minister went alone to bathe in its smooth waters. After he had bathed, and when he was just going to return to the tents, he was startled by hearing the sound of a gun. The sound came from the midst of a small grove of palm-trees close by. Alarmed, he ran back quickly to the tents: again he heard the report of a gun: and again a third time. The travellers, Arabs and all, were gathered together, expecting an enemy to rush out of the grove. But where was Suleiman? He had gone some time before into the grove of palm-trees to talk to the enemies.

Presently the traveller saw about forty Arabs leave the grove and go far away. But Suleiman came not. So the minister went into the grove to search for him, and there he found—not Suleiman—but his dead body!

There it lay on the ground, covered with blood. The minister gazed upon the dark countenance once so joyful, and he thought it looked as if the poor Arab had died in great agony. It was frightful to observe the number of his wounds. Three balls had been shot into his body by the gun which went off three times. Three great cuts had been made in his head; his neck was almost cut off from his head, and his hand from his arm! How suddenly was the proud Arab laid low in the dust! All his delights were perished forever. Suleiman had been promised a new dress of gay colors at the end of the journey; but he would never more gird a shawl round his active frame, or fold a turban round his swarthy brow. The Arabs wrapped their beloved master in a loose garment, and placing him on his beautiful camel, they went in deep grief to a hill at a little distance. There they buried him. They dug no grave; but they made a square tomb of large loose stones, and laid the dead body in the midst, and then covered it with more stones. There Suleiman sleeps in the desert. But the day shall come when "the earth shall disclose her blood, and shall no more cover her slain:" and then shall the blood of Suleiman and his slain body be uncovered, and his murderer brought to judgment.*

* Extracted chiefly from "The Pastor's Memorial," by the Rev. G. Fisk. Published by R. Carter & Brothers.

Turkey in Asia.

Is there a Turkey in Asia as well as a Turkey in Europe?

Yes, there is; and it is governed by the same sultan, and filled by the same sort of persons. All the Turks are Mahomedans.

You may know a Mahomedan city at a distance. When we look at a Christian city we see the steeples and spires of churches; but when we look at a Mahomedan city we see rising above the houses and trees the domes and minarets of mosques. What are domes and minarets? A dome is the round top of a mosque: and the minarets are the tall slender towers. A minaret is of great use to the Mahomedans.

Do you see the little narrow gallery outside the minaret. There is a man standing there. He is calling people to say their prayers. He calls so loud that all the people below can hear, and the sounds he utters are like sweet music. But would it not make you sad to hear them when you remembered what he was telling people to do? To pray to the god of Mahomet, not to the God and Father of the Lord Jesus Christ; but to a false god: to no God. This man goes up the dark narrow stairs winding inside the minaret five times a day: first he goes as soon as the sun rises, then at noon, next in the afternoon, then at sunset, and last of all in the night. Ascending and descending those steep stairs is all his business, and it is hard work, and fatigues him very much.

In the court of the mosque there is a fountain. There every one washes bef re he goes into the mosque to repeat his prayers, thinking to please God by clean hands inst ad of a clean heart. Inside the mosque there are no pews or benches, but only mats and carpets spread on the floor. There the worshippers kneel and touch the ground with their foreheads. The minister of the mosque is called the Imam. He stands in a niche in the wall, with his back to the people, and repeats prayers.

But he is not the preacher. The sheikh, or chief man of the town, preaches; not on Sunday, but on Friday. He sits on a high place and talks to the people—not about pardon and peace, and heaven and holiness—but about the duty of washing their hands before prayers, and of bowing down to the ground, and such vain services.

In the mosque there are two rows of very large wax candles, much higher than a man, and as thick as his arm, and they are lighted at night.

It is considered right to go to the mosque for prayers five times a day; but very few Mahomedans go so often. Wherever people may be, they are expected to kneel down and repeat their prayers, whether in the house or in the street. But very few do so. While they pray, Mahomedans look about all the time, and in the midst speak to any one, and then go on again; for their hearts are not in their prayers; they do not worship in spirit and in truth.

There are no images or pictures in the mosques, because Mahomet forbid his followers to worship idols. There are Korans on reading stands in various parts of the mosque for any one to read who pleases.

The people leave their red slippers at the door, keeping on their yellow boots only; but they do not uncover their heads as Christians do.

Was Christ ever known in this Mahomedan land? Yes, long before he was known in England. Turkey in Asia used to be called Asia Minor, (or Asia the less,) and there it was that Paul the apostle was born, and there he preached and turned many to Christ. But at last the Christians began to worship images, and the fierce Turks came and turned the churches into mosques. This was the punishment God sent the Christians for breaking his law. In some of the mosques you may see the marks of the pictures which the Christians painted on the walls, and which the Turks nearly scraped off.

How dreadful it would be if our churches should ever be turned into mosques! May God never send us this heavy punishment.

ARMENIA.

One corner of Turkey in Asia is called Armenia. There are many high mountains in Armenia, and one of them you would like to see very much. It is the mountain on which Noah's ark rested after the flood. I mean Ararat.*

It is a very high mountain with two peaks; and its highest peak is always covered with snow. People say that no one ever climbed to the top of that peak. I should think Noah's ark rested on a lower part of the mountain between the two peaks, for it would have been very cold for Noah's family on the snow-

* It is remarkable that this mountain lies at the point where three great empires meet, namely, Russia, Persia, and Turkey.

covered peak, and it would have been very difficult for them to get down. How pleasant it must be to stand on the side of Ararat, and to think, "Here my great father Noah stood, and my great mother, Noah's wife; here they saw the earth in all its greenness, just washed with the waters of the flood, and here they rejoiced and praised God."

I am glad to say that all the Armenians are not Mahomedans. Many are Christians, but, alas! they know very little about Christ except his name. I will tell you a short anecdote to show how ignorant they are.

Once a traveller went to see an old church in Armenia called the Church of Forty Steps, because there are forty steps to reach it: for it is built on the steep banks of a river.

The traveller found the churchyard full of boys. This churchyard was their school-room. And what were their books? The grave-stones that lay flat upon the ground. Four priests were teaching the boys. These priests wore black turbans; while Turkish Imams wear white turbans. One of these Armenian priests led the traveller to an upper room, telling him he had something very wonderful to show him. What could it be? The priest went to a niche in the wall and took out of it a bundle; then untied a silk handkerchief, and then another, and then another; till he had untied twenty-five silk handkerchiefs. What was the precious thing so carefully wrapped up? It was a New Testament.

It is a precious book indeed: but it ought to be read, and not wrapped up. The priest praised it, saying, "This is a wonderful book; it has often been laid upon sick persons, and has cured them." Then a poor old man, bent and tottering, pressed forward to kiss the book, and to rub his heavy head. This was worshipping the *book*, instead of Him who wrote it.

An Armenian village looks like a number of mole-hills: for the dwellings are holes dug in the ground with low stone walls round the holes; the roof is made of branches of trees and heaps of earth. There are generally two rooms in the hole—one for the family, and one for the cattle.

A traveller arrived one evening at such a village; and he was pleased to see fruit-trees overshadowing the hovels, and women, without veils, spinning cotton under their shadow. But he was not pleased with the room where he was to sleep. The way lay through a long dark passage under ground; and the room was filled with cattle: there was no window nor chimney. How dark and hot it was! Yet it was too damp to sleep out of doors, because a large lake was near; therefore he wrapped his cloak around him, and lay upon the ground; but he could not sleep because of the stinging of insects, and the trampling of cattle: and glad he was in the morning to breathe again the fresh air.

Rich Armenians have fine houses. Once a traveller dined with a rich Armenian. The dinner was served up in a tray, and placed on a low stool, while the company sat on the ground. One dish after another was served up till the traveller was tired of tasting them. But there was not only too much to *eat;* there was also too much to *drink*. Rakee, a kind of brandy, was handed about; and afterwards a musician came in and played and sang to amuse the company. In Turkey there is neither playing, nor singing, nor drinking spirits. The Turks think themselves much better than Christians. "For," say they, "we drink less and pray more." They do not know that real Christians are not fond of drinking, and are fond of praying; only *they* pray more in *secret*, and the Turks more in *public*.

KURDISTAN.

The fiercest of all the people in Asia are the Kurds.

They are the terror of all who live near them.

Their dwellings are in the mountains; there some live in villages, and some in black tents, and some in strong castles. At night they rush down from the mountains upon the people in the valleys, uttering a wild yell, and brandishing their swords. They enter the houses, and begin to pack up the things they find, and to place them on the backs of their mules and asses, while they drive away the cattle of the poor people; and if any one attempts to resist them, they kill him. You may suppose in what terror the poor villagers live in the valleys. They keep a man to watch all night, as well as large dogs; and they build a strong tower in the midst of the village where they run to hide themselves when they are afraid.

The reason why the Armenians live in holes in the ground is because they hope the Kurds may not find out where they are.

Those Kurds who live in tents often move from place to place. The black tents are folded up and placed on the backs of mules; and a large kettle is slung upon the end of the tent-pole. The men and women drive the herds and flocks, while the children and the chickens ride upon the cows.

The Kurds have thin, dark faces, hooked noses, and black eyes, with a fierce and malicious look.

They are of the Mahomedan religion, and the call to prayers may be heard in the villages of these robbers and murderers.

MESOPOTAMIA.

This country is part of Turkey in Asia. It lies between two very famous rivers, the Tigris and the Euphrates, often spoken of in the Bible. The word Mesopotamia means "between rivers." It was between these rivers that faithful Abraham lived when God first called him to be his friend. Should you not like to see that country? It is now full of ruins. The two most ancient cities in the world were built on the Tigris and Euphrates.

Nineveh was on the Tigris.

What a city that was at the time Jonah preached there! Its walls were so thick that three chariots could go on the top all abreast.

But what is Nineveh now? Look at those green mounds. Under those heaps of rubbish lies Nineveh.

A traveller has been digging among those mounds, and has found the very throne of the kings of Nineveh, and the images of winged bulls and lions which adorned the palace. God overthrew Nineveh because it was wicked.

There is another ancient city lying in ruins on the Euphrates, it is Babylon the Great.

There are nothing but heaps of bricks to be seen where once proud Babylon stood. Where are now the streets fifteen miles long? Where are the hanging gardens? gardens one above the other, the wonder of the world? Where is now the temple of Belus, (or of Babel, as some think,) with its golden statue? All, all are now crumbled into rubbish. God has destroyed Babylon as he said.

There are dens of wild beasts among the ruins. A traveller saw some bones of a sheep in one, the remains, he supposed, of a lion's dinner; but he did not like to go further into the den to see who dwelt there. Owls and bats fill all the dark places. But no men live there, though human bones are often found scattered about, and they turn into dust as soon as they are touched.

There is now a great city in Mesopotamia, called Bagdad. In Babylon no sound is heard but the howlings of wild beasts; in Bagdad men may be heard screaming and hallooing from morning to night. The drivers of the camels and the mules shout as they press through the narrow crooked streets, and even the ladies riding on white donkeys, and attended by black slaves, scream and halloo.

In summer it is so hot in Bagdad that people during the day live in rooms under ground, and sleep on their flat roofs at night.

It is curious to see the people who have been sleeping on the roof get up in the morning. First they roll up their mattrasses, their coverlids, and pillows, and put them in the house. The children cannot fold up theirs, but their mothers or black slaves do it for them. The men repeat their prayers, and then drink a cup of coffee, which their wives present to them. The wives kneel as they offer the cup to their lords, and stand with their hands crossed while their lords are drinking, then kneel down again to receive the cup, and to kiss their lords' hand. Then the men take their pipes, and lounge on their cushions, while the women say their prayers. And when do the children say their prayers? Never. They know only of Mahomet; they know not the Saviour who said, "Suffer little children to come unto me."

Persia.

Is this country mentioned in the Bible? Yes; we read of Cyrus, the king of Persia. Isaiah spoke of him before he was born, and called him by his name. See chapter xlv.

Persia is now a Mahomedan country. The Turks, you remember, are Mahomedans too. Perhaps you think those two nations, the Turks and the Persians, must agree well together, as they are of the same religion. Far from it. No nations hate one another more than Turks and Persians do; and the reason is, that though they both believe in Mahomet, they disagree about his son-in law, Ali. The Persians are very fond of him, and keep a day of mourning in memory of his death; whereas the Turks do not care for Ali at all.

But is this a reason why they should hate one another so much?

Even in their common customs the Persians differ from the Turks. The Turks sit cross-legged on the ground; the Persians sit upon their heels. Which way of sitting should you prefer? I think you would find it more comfortable to sit like a Turk.

The Turks sit on sofas and lean against cushions; the Persians sit on carpets and lean against the wall. I know you would prefer the Turkish fashion. The Turks drink coffee without either milk or sugar; the Persians drink tea with sugar, though without milk. The Turks wear turbans; the Persians wear high caps of black lamb's-wool.

Not only are their *customs* different, but their *characters*. The Turks are grave and the Persians lively. The Turks are silent, the Persians talkative. The Turks are rude, the Persians polite. Now I am sure you like the Persians better than the Turks. But wait a little—the Turks are very proud; the Persians are very deceitful. An old Persian was heard to say, "We all tell lies whenever we can." The Persians are not even ashamed when their falsehoods are found out. When they sell they ask too much; when they make promises they break them. In short, it is impossible to trust a Persian.

The Turks obey Mahomet's laws; they pray five times a day, and drink no wine. But the Persians seldom repeat their prayers, and they do drink wine, though Mahomet has forbidden it. In short, the Persian seems to have no idea of right and wrong. The judges do not give right judgment, but take bribes. The soldiers live by robbing the poor people, for the king pays them no wages, but leaves them to get food as they can; and so the poor people often build their cottages in little nooks in the valleys, where they hope the soldiers will not see them.

THE COUNTRY.—Persia is a high country and a dry country. There are high mountains and wide plains; but there are very few rivers and running brooks, because there is so little rain. However, in some places the Persians have cut canals, and planted willow-trees by their side. Rice will not grow well in such a dry country, but sheep find it very pleasant and wholesome. The hills are covered over with flocks, and the shepherds may be seen leading their sheep and carrying the very young lambs in their arms. This is a sight which reminds us of the good Shepherd: for it is written of Jesus, "He gathered the lambs in his arms."

The sweetest of all flowers grows abundantly in Persia—I mean the rose. The air is filled with its fragrance. The people pluck the rose leaves and dry them in the sun, as we dry hay. How pleasant it must be for children in the spring to play among the heaps of rose-leaves. Once a traveller went to breakfast with a Persian Prince, and he found the company seated upon a heap of rose-leaves, with a carpet spread over it. Afterwards the rose-leaves were sent to the distillers, to be made into rose-water.

Persian cats are beautiful creatures, with fur as soft as silk.

The best melons in the world grow in Persia.

The three chief materials for making clothes are all to be found there in abundance. I mean wool, cotton, and silk. You have heard already of the Persian sheep; so you see there is wool. Cotton trees also abound. Women and children may be seen picking the nuts which contain the little pieces of cotton. There are mulberry-trees also to feed the numerous silk worms.

Poor People.—The villages where the poor live are miserable places. The houses are of mud, not placed in rows, but straggling, with dirty narrow paths winding between them.

In summer the poor people sleep on the roofs; for the roofs are flat, and covered with earth, with low walls on every side to prevent the sleepers falling off. Here the Persians spread their carpets to lie upon at night.

Winter does not last long in Persia, yet while it lasts it is cold. Then the poor, instead of sleeping on their roofs, sleep in a very curious warm bed. In the middle of each cottage there is a round hole in the floor, where the fire burns. In the evening the fire goes out, but the hot cinders remain. The Persians place over it a low round table, and then throw a large coverlid over the table, and all round about. Under this coverlid the family lie at night, their heads peeping out, and their feet against the warm fire-place underneath. This the Persians call a comfortable bed.

The poor wear dirty and ragged clothes, and the children may be seen crawling about in the dust, and looking like little pigs. Yet in one respect the Persians are very clean; they bathe often. In every village there is a large bath.

The poor people have animals of various kinds—a few sheep, or goats, or cows. In the day one man takes them all out to feed. In the evening he brings them back to the village, and the animals of their own accord go home to their own stables. Each cow and each sheep knows where she will get food and a place to sleep in. The prophet Isaiah said truly, "The ass knoweth his owner, and the ox his master's crib; but Israel doth not know, my people doth not consider."

THE PERSIAN LADIES.—They wrap themselves up in a large dark blue wrapper, and in this dress they walk out where they please. No one who meets them can tell who they are.

And where do these women go? Chiefly to the bath, where they spend much of their time drinking coffee and smoking. There too they try to make themselves handsome by blackening their eyebrows and dyeing their hair. Sometimes the ladies walk to the burial-grounds, and wander about for hours among the graves. When they are at home they employ themselves in making pillau and sherbet. Pillau is made of rice and butter; sherbet is made of juice mixed with water.

The ladies have a sitting-room to themselves. One side of it is all lattice-work, and this makes it cool. At night they spread their carpets on the floor to sleep upon, and in the day they keep them in a lumber-room.

Persian Inns.—They are very uncomfortable places. There are a great many small cells made of mud, built all round a large court. These cells are quite empty, and paved with stone. The only comfortable room is over the door-way of the court, and the first travellers who arrive are sure to settle in the room over the door-way.

Once an English traveller arrived at a Persian inn with his two servants. All three were very ill and in great pain, from having travelled far over burning plains and steep mountains.

But as the room over the door-way was occupied, they were forced to go into a little cold damp cell. As there was no door to the cell, they hung up a rag to keep out the chilling night air, and they placed a pan of coals in the midst. Many Persians came and peeped into the cell; and seeing the sick men looking miserable as they lay on their carpets, the unfeeling creatures laughed at them, and no one would help them or give them anything to eat. The travellers bought some bread and grapes at the bazaar, but these were not fit food for sick men, but it was all they could get. At last a Persian merchant heard of their distress; and he came to see them every day, bringing them warm milk and wholesome food: when they were well enough to be moved, he took them to his own house, and nursed them with the greatest care.

Who was this kind merchant? Not a Mahomedan, but of the religion of the fire worshippers, or Parsees. Was he not like the good Samaritan of whom we read in the New Testament? O that Bah ram, the merchant, might know the true God!

PILGRIMS AND BEGGARS.—Very often you may see a large company of Pilgrims, some on foot, and some mounted on camels, horses, and asses. They are returning from Mecca, the birth-place of Mahomet. What good have they got by their pilgrimage? None at all. They think they are grown very holy, but they make such an uproar at the inns by quarrelling and fighting when they are travelling home, that no one can bear to be near them.

There is a set of beggars called dervishes. They call themselves very holy, and think people are bound to give money to such holy men. They are so bold that sometimes they refuse to leave a place till some money has been given.

Once a dervish stopped a long while before the house of the English ambassador, and refused to go away. But a plan was thought of to *make* him go away.

The dervish was sitting in a little niche in the wall. The ambassador ordered his servants to build up bricks to shut the dervish in. The men began to build, yet the dervish would not stir, till the bricks came up as high as his chin: then he began to be frightened, and said he would rather go away.

THE KING OF PERSIA.—He is called King of Kings. What a name for a man! It is the title of God alone. The king sits on a marble throne, and his garments sparkle with jewels of dazzling brightness. The walls of his state-chamber are covered with looking-glasses. One side of the room opens into a court adorned with flowers and fountains. Great part of his time is spent in amusements, such as hunting and shooting, writing verses, and hearing stories. He keeps a man called a story-teller, and he will never hear the same story repeated twice. It gives the man a great deal of trouble to find new stories every day. The king keeps jesters, who make jokes; and he has mimics, who play antics to make him laugh. He dines at eight in the evening from dishes of pure gold. No one is allowed to dine with him; but two of his little boys wait upon him, and his physician stands by to advise him not to eat too much.

Do you think he is happy in all his grandeur? Judge for yourself.

All his golden dishes come up covered and sealed. Why? For fear of poison. There is a chief officer in the kitchen who watches the cook, to see that he puts no poison into the food: and he seals up the dishes before they are taken to the king, in order that the servants may not put in poison as they are carrying them along. In what fear this great king lives! He cannot trust his own servants.

TEHERAN.—This is the royal city. It is built in a barren plain, and is exceedingly hot, as the hills around keep off the air. It is a mean city, for it is chiefly built of mud huts.

The king's palace is called the "Ark," and is a very strong as well as grand place.*

* Extracted chiefly from Southgate's Travels.

China.

There is no country in the world like China.

How different it is from Persia, where there are so few people; whereas China is crowded with inhabitants!

How different it is from England, where the people are instructed in the Bible, whereas China is full of idols.

China is a heathen country; yet it is not a savage country, for the people are quiet, and orderly, and industrious.

It would be hard for a child to imagine what a great multitude of people there are in China.

If you were to sit by a clock, and if all the Chinese were to pass before you one at a time, and if you were to count one at each tick of the clock, and if you were never to leave off counting day or night—how long do you think it would be before you had counted all the Chinese?

Twelve years. O what a vast number of people

there must be in China! In all, there are about three hundred and sixty millions! If all the people in the world were collected together, out of every three one would be a Chinese. How sad it is to think that this immense nation knows not God, nor his glorious Son!

There are too many people in China, for there is not food enough for them all; and many are half-starved.

FOOD.—The poor can get nothing but rice to eat and water to drink; except now and then they mix a little pork or salt fish with their rice. Any sort of meat is thought good; even a hash of rats and snakes, or a mince of earth-worms. Cats and dogs' flesh are considered as nice as pork, and cost as much.

An Englishman was once dining with a Chinaman, and he wished to know what sort of meat was on his plate. But he was not able to speak Chinese. How then could he ask? He thought of a way. Looking first at his plate, and then at the Chinaman, he said, "Ba-a-a," meaning to ask, "Is this mutton?" The Chinaman understood the question, and immediately replied, "Bow-wow," meaning to say, "It is puppy-dog." You will wish to know whether the Englishman went on eating; but I cannot tell you this.

While the poor are in want of food, the rich eat a great deal too much. A Chinese feast in a rich man's house lasts for hours. The servants bring in one course after another, till a stranger wonders when the last course will come. The food is served up in a curious way; not on dishes, but in small basins—for all the meats are swimming in broth. Instead of a knife and fork, each person has a pair of chop-sticks, which are something like knitting-needles; and with these he cleverly fishes up the floating morsels, and pops them into his mouth. There are spoons of china for drinking the broth.

You will be surprised to hear that the Chinese are very fond of eating birds' nests. Do not suppose that they eat magpies' nests, which are made of clay and sticks, or even little nests of moss and clay; the nests they eat are made of a sort of gum. This gum comes out of the bird's mouth, and is shining and transparent, and the nest sticks fast to the rock. These nests are something like our jelly, and must be very nourishing.

The Chinese like nothing cold; they warm all their food, even their wine. For they have wine, not made of grapes, but of rice, and they drink it, not in glasses, but in cups. Tea, however, is the most common drink; for China is the country where tea grows.

The hills are covered with shrubs bearing a white flower, a little like a white rose. They are tea-plants.

The leaves are picked; each leaf is rolled up with the finger, and dried on a hot iron plate.

The Chinese do not keep all the tea-leaves; they pack up a great many in boxes, and send them to distant lands. In England and in Russia there is a tea-kettle in every cottage. Some of the Chinese are so very poor that they cannot buy new tea-leaves, but only tea-leaves which are sold in shops. I do not think in England poor people would buy old tea-leaves. Some very poor Chinese use fern-leaves instead of tea-leaves.

The Chinese do not make tea in the same way that we do. They have no teapot, or milk-jug, or sugar-basin. They put a few tea-leaves in a cup, pour hot water on them, and then put a cover on the cup till the tea is ready. Whenever you pay a visit in China a cup of tea is offered.

APPEARANCE.—The Chinese are not at all like the other natives of Asia. The Turks and Arabs are fine-looking men, but the Chinese are poor-looking creatures. You have seen their pictures on their boxes of tea, for they are fond of drawing pictures of themselves.

Their complexion is rather yellow, but many of the ladies, who keep in doors, are rather fair. They have black hair, small dark eyes, broad faces, flat noses, and high cheek-bones. In general they are short. The men like to be stout; and the rich men are stout: the fatter they are, the more they are admired : but the women like to be slender.

A Chinaman does not take off his cap in company, and he has a good reason for it: his head is close shaven: only a long piece behind is allowed to grow, and this grows down to his heels, and is plaited. He wears a long dark blue gown, with loose hanging sleeves. His shoes are clumsy, turned up at the toes in an ugly manner, and the soles are white. The Chinese have more trouble in whitening their shoes than we have in blacking ours.

A Chinese lady wears a loose gown like a Chinaman's; but she may be known by her head-dress, her baby feet, and her long nails. Her hair is tied up, and decked with artificial flowers; and sometimes a little golden bird, sparkling with jewels, adorns her forehead. Her feet are not bigger than those of a child of five years old; because, when she was five, they were cruelly bound up to prevent them from growing. She suffered much pain all her childhood, and now she trips about as if she were walking on tiptoes. A little push would throw her down. As she walks she moves from side to side like a ship in the water, for she cannot walk firmly with such small feet. The Chinese are so foolish as to admire these small feet, and to call them the "golden lilies." As for her finger-nails, they are seldom seen, for a Chinese lady hides her hands in her long sleeves; but the nails on the left hand are very long, and are like bird's claws. The nails on the right hand are not so long, in order that the lady may be able to tinkle on her music, to embroider, and to weave silk.

The gentlemen are proud of having one long nail on the little finger, to show that they do not labor like the poor, for if they did, the nail would break. Men in China wear necklaces and use fans.

What foolish customs I have described. Surely you will not think the Chinese a wise people, though very *clever*, as you will soon find.

Men and women dress in black, or in dark colors, such as blue and purple; the women sometimes dress in pink or green. Great people dress in red, and the royal family in yellow. When you see a person all in white, you may know he is in mourning. A son dresses in white for three years after he has lost one of his parents.

Houses.—See that lantern hanging over the gate. The light is rather dim, because the sides are made of silk instead of glass. What is written upon the lantern? The master's name. The gateway leads into a court into which many rooms open. There are not doors to all the rooms; to some there are only curtains. Curtains are used instead of doors in many hot countries, because of their coolness; but the furniture of the Chinese rooms is quite different from the furniture of Turkish and Persian rooms. The Chinese sit on chairs as we do, and have high tables like ours: and they sleep on bedsteads, yet their beds are not like ours, for instead of a mattrass there is nothing but a mat.

Instead of pictures, the Chinese adorn their rooms with painted lanterns, and with pieces of white satin, on which sentences are written: they have also book-cases and china jars. But they have no fire-places, for they never need a fire to keep themselves warm: the sun shining in at the south windows makes the rooms tolerably warm in winter; and in summer the weather is very hot. The Chinese in winter put on one coat over the other till they feel warm enough. In the north of China it is so cold in winter that the place where the bed stands (which is a recess in the wall) is heated by a furnace underneath, and the whole family sit there all day crowded together.

The Chinese houses have not so many stories as ours; in the towns there is one floor above the ground floor, but in the country there are no rooms up stairs.

It would amuse you to see a Chinese country house. There is not one large house, but a number of small buildings like summer-houses, and long galleries running from one to another. One of these summer-houses is in the middle of a pond, with a bridge leading to it. In the pond there are gold and silver fish; for these beautiful fishes, often kept in glass bowls in England, came first from China. By the sides of the garden walls large cages are placed; in one may be seen some gold and silver pheasants, in another a splendid peacock; in another a gentle stork, and in another an elegant little deer. There is often a grove of mulberry-trees in the garden, and in the midst of the grove houses made of bamboo, for rearing silk-worms. It is the delight of the ladies to feed these curious worms. None but very quiet people are fit to take care of them, for a loud noise would kill them. Gold and silver fish also cannot bear much noise.

In every large house in China there is a room called the Hall of Ancestors. There the family worship their dead parents and grand-parents, and great-grand-parents, and those who lived still further back. There are no images to be seen in the Hall of Ancestors, but there are tablets with names written upon them. The family bow down before the tablets, and burn incense and gold paper! What a foolish service! What good can incense and paper do to the dead? And what good can the dead do to their children? How is it that such clever people as the Chinese are so foolish!

RELIGION.—You have heard already that the Chinese worship the dead.

Who taught them this worship?

It was a man named Confucius, who lived a long while ago. This Confucius was a very wise man. From his childhood he was very fond of sitting alone thinking, instead of playing with other children. When he was fourteen he began to read some old books that had been written not long after the time of Noah. In these books he found very many wise sentences, such as Noah may have taught his children. The Chinese had left off reading these wise books, and were growing more and more foolish.* Confucius,

* These are some of the sentences written in the old books: "Never say, There is no one who sees me, for there is a wise Spirit who sees all."

"Man no longer has what he had before the fall, and he has brought his children into his misery. O! Heaven, you only can help us. Wipe away the stains of the father, and save his children."

"Never speak but with great care. Do not say, It is only a single word. Remember that no one has the keeping of your heart and tongue but you."

These sentences are like some verses in the Psalms and

when he was grown up, tried to persuade his countrymen to attend to the old books. There were a few men who became his scholars, and who followed him about from place to place. They might be seen sitting under a tree, listening to the words of Confucius.

Confucius was a very tall man with a long black beard and a very high forehead.

Had he known the true God, how much good he might have done to the Chinese; but as it was he only tried to make them happy in this world. He himself confessed that he knew nothing about the other world. He gave very good advice about respect due to parents; but he gave very bad advice about worship due to them after they were dead.

Was he a good man? Not truly good; for he did not love God; neither did he act right: for he was very unkind to his wife, and quite cast her off. Yet he used to talk of going to other countries to teach the people. It would have been a happy thing for him, if he had gone as far as Babylon; for a truly wise man lived there, even Daniel the prophet. From him he might have learned about the promised Sa-

Proverbs; and, it may be, they were spoken first by some holy men of old.

Here is one more remarkable than all:—

"God hates the proud, and is kind to the humble."

viour, and life everlasting. But Confucius never left China.

He was ill-treated by many of the rich and great, and he was so poor that rice was generally his only food. When he was dying he felt very unhappy, as well he might, when he knew not where he was going. He said to his followers just before his death, "The kings refuse to follow my advice; and since I am of no use on earth, it is best that I should leave it." As soon as he was dead, people began to respect him highly, and even to worship him. At this day, though Confucius died more than two thousand years ago, there is a temple to his honor in every large city, and numbers of beasts are offered up to him in sacrifice. There are thousands of people descended from him, and they are treated with great honor as the children of Confucius, and one of them is called kong or duke.

There is another religion in China besides the religion of Confucius, and a much worse religion. About the same time that Confucius lived, there was a man called La-on-tzee. He was a great deceiver, as you will see. He pretended that he could make people completely happy. There were three things he said he would do for them: first, he would make them rich by turning stone into gold; next, he would prevent their being hurt by swords or by fire through charms

THE PRIESTS OF LA-ON-TZEE. p. 83.

he could give them; and, last of all, he could save them from death by a drink he knew how to prepare.

What an awful liar this man must have been! Yet many people believed in him, and still believe in him. There are now priests of La-on-tzee, and once a year they rush through hot cinders and pretend they are not hurt. You will wonder their tricks are not found out, seeing they cannot give any one the drink to keep them from dying. It is indeed wonderful that any one can believe these deceitful priests.

Their religion is called the "*Taou*" sect. Taou means reason. The name of folly would be a better title for such a religion.

There is a *third* religion in China. It is the sect of Buddha.* This Buddha was a man who once

* The means by which the Buddhist religion entered China are remarkable. A certain Chinese emperor once read in the book of Confucius this sentence, "The true saint will be found in the West." He thought a great deal about it; at last he dreamed about it. He was so much struck by his dream that he sent two of his great lords to look for the true religion in the West. When they reached India, they found multitudes worshipping Buddha. This Buddha was a wicked man who had been born in India a thousand years before. The Chinese messengers believed all the absurd histories they heard about Buddha, and they returned to China with a book which had been written about him. Ah! had they gone as far as Canaan they might have heard Paul

pretended to be turned into a god called Fo. You see he was even worse than La-on-tzee.

Buddha pretended that he could make people happy; and his way of doing so was very strange. He told them to think of nothing, and then they would be happy. It is said that one man fixed his eyes for nine years upon a wall without looking off, hoping to grow happy at last. You can guess whether he did. There are many priests of Buddha, always busy in telling lies to the people. They recommend them to repeat the name of Buddha thousands and thousands of times, and some people are so foolish as to do this; but no one ever found any comfort from this plan.

The priests of Buddha say that their souls, when they leave their bodies, go into other bodies. This idea is enough to make a dying person very miserable. One poor man, when he was dying, was in terror because he had been told his soul would go into one of the emperor's horses. Whenever he was dropping off to sleep, he started up in a fright, fancying that he felt the blows of a cruel driver hurrying him along: for he knew how very fast the emperor's horses

and Peter preaching the Gospel. Alas! why did they go no further, and why did they go so far, only to return to China with idols!

were made to go. How different are the feelings of a dying man who knows he is going to Jesus.

He can say with joy,—

> "For me my elder brethren stay,
> And angels beckon me away,
> And Jesus bids me come."

The Buddhists are full of tricks by which to get presents out of the people.

Once a year they cause a great feast to be made, and for whom? For the poor? No. For beasts? No. For children? No. For themselves? No. You will never guess. For ghosts! The priests declare that the souls of the dead are very hungry, and that it is right to give them a feast. A number of tables are set out, spread with all kinds of dishes. No one is seen to eat, nor is any of the food eaten; but the priests say the ghosts eat the spirit of the food. When it is supposed the ghosts have finished dinner, the people scramble for the food, and take it home, and no doubt the priests get their share.

Tho dead are supplied with money as well as with food, and that is done by burning gilt paper; clothes are sent to them by cutting out paper in the shape of clothes, (only much smaller,) and by burning the article; and even houses are conveyed to the dead by making baby-houses and burning them.

As an instance of the deceits of the priests, I will tell you of two priests who once stood crying over a poor woman's gate. "What is the matter?" inquired the woman. "Do you see those ducks?" the priests replied; "our parents' souls are in them, and we are afraid lest you should eat them for supper." The foolish woman out of pity gave the ducks to the cunning priests, who promised to take great care of the precious birds; but, in fact, they ate them for their own supper.

The Buddhist priests may be known by their heads close shaven, and their black dress. The priests of Taou have their hair in a knot at the top of their heads, and they wear scarlet robes. There are no priests of Confucius; and this is a good thing.

All the religions of China are bad, but of the three the religion of Confucius is the least foolish.

There can be no doubt which of the three religions of China is the least absurd.

The religion of Taou teaches men to act like madmen.

The religion of Buddha teaches them to act like idiots.

The religion of Confucius teaches them to act like wise men, but without souls.

THE EMPEROR.—There is no emperor in the world

who has as many subjects as the Emperor of China: he has six times as many as the Emperor of Russia.

Neither is it possible for any man to be more honored than this emperor; for he is worshipped by his people like a god. He is called "The Son of Heaven," and "Ten Thousand Years;" yet he dies like every other child of earth. His sign is the dragon, and this is painted on his flags, a fit sign for one who, like Satan, makes himself a god.

Yet the emperor is also styled "Father of his people," and to show that he feels like a father, when there is a famine or plague in the land, he shuts himself up in his palace to grieve for his people; and by this means he gets the love of his subjects.

Once a year, too, this great emperor tries to encourage his people to be industrious by ploughing part of a field and sowing a little corn; and the empress sets an example to the women, by going once a year to feed silk worms and to wind the balls of silk.

The emperor wears a yellow dress, and all his relations wear yellow girdles.

But the relations of the emperor are not the most honorable people in the land: the most learned are the most honorable. Every one in China who wishes to be a great lord studies day and night. One man, that he might not fall asleep over his books, tied his long plaited tail of hair to the ceiling, and when his head nodded, his hair was pulled tight, and that woke him.

But what is it the Chinese learn with so much pains?

Chiefly the books of Confucius, and a few more; but in none of them is God made known: so that, with all his wisdom, the Chinaman is foolish still. The words of the Bible are true.

"The world by wisdom knew not God." Yet to know God is better than to know all beside.

There is a great hall in every town where all the men who wish to be counted learned meet together once a year. They are desired to write, and then to show what they have written; and then those who have written well, and without a mistake, have an honorable title given to them; and they are allowed to write another year in another greater hall; and at last the most learned are made mandarins.

What is a mandarin? He is a ruler over a town, and is counted a great man. The most learned of the mandarins are made the emperor's counsellors. There are only three of them, and they are the greatest men in all China, next to the emperor.

There are many poor men who study hard in hopes to be one of these three.

This is the greatest honor a Chinaman can obtain. But a Christian can obtain a far greater, even the honor of a crown and a throne in the presence of the Lord Jesus Christ at his coming.

The mandarins are all of the religion of Confucius, and despise the poor who worship Buddha.

ANIMALS AND TREES.—Once there were lions in China, but they have all been killed; there are still bears and tigers in the mountains and forests on the borders of the land.

There are small wild-cats, which are caught and fastened in cages, and then killed and cooked. There are tame cats, too, with soft hair and hanging ears, which are kept by ladies as pets.

There are dogs to guard the house, and they too are eaten; but as they are fed on rice only, their flesh is better than the flesh of our dogs. The dogs are so sensible that they know when the butcher is carrying away a dog that he is going to kill him, and the poor creatures come round him howling, as if begging for their brother's life.

The pig is the Chinaman's chief dish; for it can be fed on all the refuse food, and there is very little food to spare in China.

There are not many birds in China, because there is no room for trees. Only one bird sings, and she builds her nest on the ground; it is a bird often heard singing in England floating in the air,—I mean the lark.

In most parts of China men carry all the burdens, and not horses and asses.

A gentleman is carried in a chair by two men: and a mandarin by four. Yet the emperor rides on horseback.

THE THREE GREAT CITIES.

Pekin on the north.
Nankin in the middle.
Canton on the south.

Pekin is the grandest.
Nankin is the most learned.
Canton is the richest.

At Pekin is the emperor's palace. The gardens are exceedingly large, and contain hills, and lakes, and groves within the walls, besides houses for the emperor's relations.

At Nankin is the China tower. It is made of China bricks, and contains nine rooms one over the other. It is two hundred feet high, a wonderful height.

Of what use is it? Of none—of worse than none. It is a temple for Buddha, and is full of his images.

At Canton there are so many people that there is

not room for all in the land; so thousands live on the water in boats. Many have never slept a single night on the shore. The children often fall overboard, but as a hollow gourd is tied round each child's neck, they float, and are soon picked up.

For a long while the Chinese would not allow foreigners to come into their cities. A great many foreign ships came to Canton to buy tea and silk; but the traders were forbidden to enter the town, and they lived in a little island near, and built a town there called Macao.

But lately the Chinese emperor has agreed to permit strangers to come to five ports, called Shang-hae, Ning-po, Foo-choo, Amoy, and Hong-Kong.

This last port, Hong-Kong, is an island near Canton, and the English have built a city there and called it Victoria.

The Two Rivers.—There is one called Yeang-tesang, or "the Son of the Ocean." It is the largest in Asia.

The other is the Yellow River, for the soft clay mixed with the water gives it a yellow color.

Lakes.—There are immense lakes, covered with boats and fishermen.

But the best fishers are the tame cormorants, who catch fish for their masters.

THE TWO GREAT WONDERS.—The great CANAL is a wonder. It joins the two rivers; so that a Chinese can go by water from Canton to Pekin.

The great WALL is a greater wonder, but not nearly as useful as the canal.

This wall was built at the north of China to keep the Tartars out. It is one thousand five hundred miles long, twenty feet high, and twenty-five broad. But there were not soldiers enough in China to keep the enemies out, and the Tartars came over the wall.

The Emperor of China is a Tartar.

The Empress does not have small feet, like the Chinese.

It is the Tartars who forced the Chinese to shave their heads, for they used to tie up their hair in a knot at the top of their heads. Many of the Chinese preferred losing their heads to their hair. Was it not cruel to cut off their heads, merely because they would not shave them? But the Tartars were very cruel to the Chinese.

KNOWLEDGE AND INVENTIONS.—We must allow that the Chinese are very clever. They found out how to print, and they found out how to make gunpowder, and they found out the use of the loadstone. What is that? A piece of steel rubbed against the loadstone will always point to the north. The Chinese found out these three things, printing, gunpowder, and the use of the loadstone, before we in Europe found them out. But they did not teach them to us; we found them out ourselves.

But there are two arts that the Chinese did teach us: how to make silk, and how to make china or porcelain. And yet I should not say they taught us; for they tried to prevent our learning their arts; but we saw their silk and their porcelain, and by degrees we learned to make them ourselves. A sly monk brought some silk-worm's eggs from China hidden in a hollow walking-stick.

LANGUAGE.—There is no other language at all like the Chinese. Instead of having letters to spell words, they have a picture for each word. I call it a picture, but it is more like a figure than a picture. The Chinese use brushes for writing instead of pens; and they rub cakes of ink on a little marble dish, first dipping them in a little water, as we dip cakes of paint. There is a hollow place in the marble dish, to hold the water. What do you think the Chinese mean by "the four precious things?" They mean the ink, the brush, the marble dish, and the water. They call them precious because they are so fond of writing. Schoolmasters are held in great honor in China, as indeed they ought to be everywhere. Yet schools in China are much like those in Turkey, more fit for parrots than children; only Chinese boys sit in chairs with desks before them, instead of sitting cross-legged on the ground, as in Turkey. They learn first to paint the words, and next to repeat lessons by heart. This they do in a loud scream; always turning their backs to their masters while they are saying their lessons to him.

The first book which children read is full of stories, with a picture on each page. Would you like to hear one of these stories?

"There was a boy of eight years old, named Umwen. His parents were so poor that they could not afford to buy a gauze curtain for their bed, to keep off the flies in summer. This boy could not bear that his parents should be bitten by the flies; so he stood by their bedside, and uncovered his little bosom and his back that the flies might bite him, instead of his parents. 'For,' said he, 'if they fill themselves with my blood, they will let my parents rest.'"

Would it be right for a little boy to behave in this way? Certainly not; for it would grieve kind parents that their little boys should be bitten. Poor little Chinese boys! They do not know about Him who was bitten by the old serpent that we might not be devoured and destroyed.

PUNISHMENT.—The Chinese are very quiet and orderly; and no wonder, because they are afraid of the great bamboo stick.

The mandarins (or rulers of towns) often sentence offenders to lie upon the ground, and to have thirty strokes of the bamboo. But the wooden collar is worse than the bamboo stick. It is a great piece of wood with a hole for a man to put his head through. The men in wooden collars are brought out of their prisons every morning, and chained to a wall, where everybody passing by can see them. They cannot feed themselves in their wooden collars, because they cannot bring their hands to their mouths; but sometimes a son may be seen feeding his father, as he stands chained to the wall. There are men also whose business it is to feed the prisoners. For great crimes men are strangled or beheaded.

Character.—A Chinaman's character cannot be known at first. You might suppose from his way of speaking that a Chinaman was very humble; because he calls himself "the worthless fellow," or "the stupid one," and he calls his son "the son of a dog;" but if you were to tell him he had an evil heart, he would be very much offended; for he only gives himself these names that he may *seem* humble. He calls his acquaintance "venerable uncle," "honorable brother." This he does to please them. The Chinese are very proud of their country, and think there is none like it. They have given it the name of the "Heavenly or Celestial Empire." They look upon foreigners as monkeys and devils. Often a woman may be heard in the streets saying to her little child, "There is a foreign devil (or a Fan Quei"). The Chinese think the English very ugly, and called them the "red-haired nation."

It must be owned that the Chinese are industrious: indeed, if they were not, they would be starved. A poor man often has to work all day up to the knees in water in the rice-field, and yet gets nothing for supper but a little rice and a few potatoes.

The ladies who can live without working are very idle, and in the winter rise very late in the morning.

Men, too, play, as children do here; flying kites is a favorite game. Dancing, however, is quite unknown.

The Chinese are very selfish and unfeeling. Beggars may be seen in the middle of the town dying, and no one caring for them, but people gambling close by.

The Chinese have an idea that after a man is dead the house must be cleansed from ghosts; so to save themselves this trouble, poor people often cast their dying relations out of their hovels into the street to die!

But in general sons treat their parents with great respect. They often keep their father's coffin in the house for three months, and a son has been known to sleep by it for three years. Relations are usually kind to each other, because they meet together in the "Hall of Ancestors" to worship the same persons. To save money they often live together, and a hundred eat at the same table.

The Chinese used to be temperate, preferring tea to wine. There are tea-taverns in the towns. How much better than our beer-shops! But lately they have begun to smoke opium. This is the juice of the white poppy, made up into dark balls. The Chinese are not allowed to have it; but the English, sad to say, sell it to them secretly. There are many opium taverns in China, where men may be seen lying on cushions snuffing up the hot opium, and puffing it out of their mouths. Those who smoke opium have sunken cheeks and trembling hands, and soon become old, foolish, and sick. Why, then, do they take opium? Many of them say they wish to leave it off, but cannot.

MISSIONARIES.—Are there any in China? Yes, many; and more are going there. But how many are wanted for so many people! Missionaries travel about China to distribute Bibles and tracts. One of them hired a rough kind of chair with two bearers. In this he went to villages among the mountains, where a white man had never been seen. The children screaming with terror ran to their mothers. The men came round him to look at his clothes and his white skin. They were much surprised at the whiteness of his hands, and they put their yellow ones close to his to see the difference. These mountaineers were kind, and brought tea and cakes to refresh the stranger.

An English lady went to China to teach little girls; for no one teaches them. She has several little creatures in her school that she saved from perishing: because the Chinese are so cruel as to leave many girl-babies to die in the streets; they say that girls are not worth the trouble of bringing up.

One cold rainy evening, Miss Aldersey heard a low wailing outside the street-door, and looking out she saw a poor babe, wrapped in coarse matting, lying on the stone pavement. She could not bear to leave it there to be devoured by famished dogs; so she kindly took it in, and brought it up.

It is a common thing to stumble over the bodies of dead babies in the streets. In England it is counted murder to kill a babe, but it is thought no harm in China. Yet the Chinese call themselves good. But when you ask a poor man where he expects to go when he dies, he replies, "To hell of course;" and he says this with a loud laugh. His reason for thinking he shall go to hell is, because he has not money enough to give to the gods; for rich people all expect to go to heaven. Mandarins especially expect to go there. If they were to read the Bible, they would see that God will punish kings, and mighty men, and great captains, and *all* who are wicked.

Cochin China.

Any one on hearing this name would guess that the country was like China; and so it is. If you were to go there you would be reminded of China by many of the customs. You would see at dinner small basins instead of plates, chop-sticks instead of knives and forks; you would have rice to eat instead of bread; and rice wine to drink instead of grape wine.

But you would not find *all* the Chinese customs in Cochin-China: for you would see the women walking about at liberty, and with large feet, that is, with feet of the natural size, and not cramped up like the "golden lilies" of China. Neither would you see the people treated as strictly in Cochin-China as in China. Beatings are not nearly as common there, and behavior is not nearly as good as in China.

The people are very different from the Chinese; for they are gay and talkative, and open and sociable, while the Chinese are just the contrary. However, they resemble the Chinese in fondness for eating. They are very fond of giving grand dinners, and sometimes provide a hundred dishes, and invite a hundred guests. A man is thought very generous who gives such grand dinners. No one in Cochin-China would think of eating his morsel alone, but every one asks those around to partake; and if any one were not to do so, he would be counted very mean. Yet the people of Cochin-China are always begging for gifts; and if they cannot get the things they ask for, they steal them. Are they generous? No, because they are covetous. It is impossible to be at the same time generous and covetous; for what goodness is there in giving away our own things, if we are wishing for other people's things?

And now let us leave the *people* and look at the *land*. It is fruitful and beautiful, being watered abundantly by fine rivers: but these rivers, flowing among lofty mountains, often overflow, and drown men and cattle. The grass of such a country must be very rich; and there are cows feeding on it; yet there is no milk or butter to be had. Why? Because the people have a foolish idea that it is wrong to milk cows.

In no country are there stronger and larger elephants; so strong and so large that one can carry thirteen persons on his back at once.

The land is full of idols: for Buddha or Fo is worshipped in Cochin-China, as he is in China.

The idols are sometimes kept in high trees, and priests may be seen mounting ladders to present offerings.

But the people are not satisfied with idols in trees; they have pocket idols, which they carry about with them everywhere.

TONQUIN.—CAMBODIA.

These two kingdoms belong to the king of Cochin-China; yet all three, Tonquin, Cambodia, and Cochin-China, pay tribute to China, and therefore they must be considered as conquered countries.

They are all very much like China in their customs. There are large cities in them all, and multitudes of people, but very little is known about them in England.

Hindostan.

This word Hindostan means "black place," for in the Persian language "hind" is "black," and "stan" is "place." You may guess, therefore, that the people in Hindostan are very dark; yet they are not quite black, and some of the ladies are only of a light brown complexion.

What a large country Hindostan is! Has it an emperor of its own, as China has? No: large as it is, it belongs to the little country called England.

How did the English get it?

They conquered it by little and little. When first they came there, they found there a Mahomedan people, called the Moguls. These Moguls had conquered Hindostan: but by degrees the English conquered them, and became masters of all the land.

There is only one small country among the mountains which has not been conquered by the English, and that place is Nepaul. It is near the Himalaya mountains. See that great chain of mountains in the north: they are the Himalaya—the highest mountains in the world. The word "him," or "hem," means snow—and snowy indeed are those mountains.

There is a great river that flows from the Himalaya called the Ganges. It flows by many mouths into the ocean; yet of all these mouths only one is deep enough for large ships to sail in; the other mouths are all choked up with sand. The deep mouth of the Ganges is called the Hoogley.

It was on the banks of the Hoogley that the first English city was built. It was built by some English merchants, and is called Calcutta. That name comes from the name of a horrible idol called Kalee, of which more will be said hereafter.

Calcutta is now a very grand city; there is the governor's palace, and there are the mansions of many rich Englishmen. It has been called "the city of palaces."

There is another great river on the other side of Hindostan called the Indus. It was from that river that Hindostan got the name of India, or the East Indies.

VILLAGES.—Calcutta is built on a large plain called Bengal. Dotted about this plain are many villages. At a distance they look prettier than English villages, for they are overshadowed with thick trees; but they are wretched places to live in. The huts are scarcely big enough to hold human creatures, nor strong enough to bear the pelting of the storm. When you enter them you will find neither floor nor window, and very little furniture; neither chair, nor table, nor bed —nothing but a large earthen bottle for fetching water, a smaller one for drinking, a basket for clothes, a few earthen pans, a few brass plates, and a mat.

A Hindoo is counted very rich who has procured a wooden bedstead to place his mat upon, and a wooden trunk, with a lock and key, to contain his clothes; such a man is considered to have a well-furnished house.

As you pass through the villages, you may see groups of men sitting under the trees smoking their pipes, while children, without clothes, are rolling in the dust, and sporting with the kids. Prowling about the villages are hungry dogs and whining jackalls, seeking for bones and offal; but the children are too much used to these creatures to be afraid of them. Hovering in the air are crows and kites, ready to secure any morsel they can see, or even to snatch the food, if they can, out of the children's little hands.

What a confused noise do you hear as you pass along! barking, whining, and squalling, loud laughing, and incessant chattering. It is a heathen village, and the sweet notes of praise to God are never sung there.

Yet in every village there is a little temple with an idol, and a priest to take the idol, to lay it down to sleep, and to offer it food, which he eats himself.

The poor people bring the food for the idol with flowers, and place it at the door of the temple.

APPEARANCE.—The Hindoos are pleasing in their appearance, for their features are well-formed, their teeth are white, and their eyes have a soft expression. The women take much pains to dress their long black hair, which is soft as silk: they gather it up in a knot at their heads, and crown it with flowers. They have no occasion for a needle to make their dresses, as they are all in one piece. They wind a long strip of white muslin (called a saree) round their bodies, and fold it over their heads like a veil, and then they are full dressed, except their ornaments, and with these they load themselves; glass rings of different colors on their arms, silver rings on their fingers and toes, and gold rings in their ears, and a gold ring in their nose.

The men wear a long strip of calico twisted closely round their bodies, and another thrown loosely over their shoulders; but this last they cast off when they are at work: it is their upper garment. On their heads they wear turbans, and on their feet sandals.

The clothes of both men and women are generally white or pink, or white bordered with red.

FOOD.—The most common food is rice; and with this curry is often mixed to give it a relish. What is curry? It is a mixture of herbs, spices, and oil.

Very poor people cannot afford to eat either rice or curry; and they eat some coarse grain instead. A lady who made a feast for the poor provided nothing but rice, and she found that it was thought as good as roast beef and plum pudding are thought in England. The day after the feast some of the poor creatures came to pick up the grains of rice that were fallen upon the ground.

The rich Hindoos eat mutton and venison, but not beef; this they think it wicked to eat, because they worship bulls and cows.

A favorite food is clarified butter, called "ghee," white rancid stuff, kept in skin bottles to mix with curry.

Water is the general drink, and there could not be a better. Yet there are intoxicating drinks, and some of the Hindoos have learned to love them, from seeing the English drink too much. What a sad thing that Christians should set a bad example to heathens!

PRODUCTIONS.—There are many beautiful trees in

India never seen in England, and many nice fruits never tasted here.

The palm-tree, with its immense leaves, is the glory of India. These leaves are very useful; they form the roof, the umbrella, the bed, the plate, and the writing-paper of the Hindoo.

The most curious tree in India is the banyan, because one tree grows into a hundred. How is that? The branches hang down, touch the ground, strike root there, and spring up into new trees—joined to the old. Under an aged banyan there is shade for a large congregation. Seventy thousand men might sit beneath its boughs.

There is a sort of grass which grows a hundred feet high, and becomes hard like wood. It is called the bamboo. The stem is hollow like a pipe, and is often used as a water-pipe. It serves also for posts for houses, and for poles for carriages.

There are abundance of nice fruits in India; and of these the mangoe is the best. You might mistake it for a pear when you saw it, but not when you tasted it. Pears cannot grow in India; the sun is too hot for grapes and oranges, excepting on the hills.

The chief productions of India are rice and cotton; rice is the food, and cotton is the clothing of the Hindoo: and quantities of these are sent to England, for though we have wheat for food, we want rice too; and though we have wool for clothing, we want cotton too.

RELIGION.—There is no nation that has so many gods as the Hindoos. What do you think of three hundred and thirty millions! There are not so many people in Hindostan as that. No one person can know the names of all these gods; and who would wish to know them? Some of them are snakes, and some are monkeys!

The chief god of all is called Brahm. But, strange to say, no one worships him. There is not an image of him in all India.

And why not? Because he is too great, the Hindoos say, to think of men on earth. He is always in a kind of sleep. What would be the use of worshipping him?

Next to him are three gods, and they are part of Brahm.

Their names are—

I. Brahma, the Creator.

II. Vishnoo, the Preserver.

III. Sheeva, the Destroyer.

Which of these should you think men ought to worship the most? Not the destroyer. Yet it is *him* they do worship the most. Very few worship Brahma the creator. And why not? Because the Hindoos think he can do no more for them than he has done; and they do not care about thanking him.

Vishnoo, the preserver, is a great favorite; because it is supposed that he bestows all manner of gifts. The Hindoos say he has been *nine* times upon the earth; first as a fish, then as a tortoise, a man, a lion, a boar, a dwarf, a giant; *twice* as a warrior, named Ram, and once as a thief, named Krishna. They say he will come again as a conquering king, riding on a white horse. Is it not wonderful they should say that? It reminds one of the prophecy in Rev. xix. about Christ's second coming. Did the Hindoos hear that prophecy in old time? They may have heard it, for the apostle Thomas once preached in India, at least we believe he did.

Why do the people worship Sheeva the destroyer? Because they hope that if they gain his favor, they shall not be destroyed by him. They do not know that none can save from the destroyer but God.

The Hindoos make images of their gods. Brahma is represented as riding on a goose; Vishnoo on a creature half-bird and half-man; and Sheeva on a bull.

Sheeva's image looks horribly ferocious with the tiger-skin and the necklace of skulls and snakes; but Sheeva's *wife* is far fiercer than himself. Her name is

Kalee. Her whole delight is said to be in blood. Those who wish to please her, offer up the blood of beasts; but those who wish to please her still more, offer up their own blood.

Her great temple, called Kalee Ghaut, is near Calcutta. There is a great feast in her honor once a year at that temple. Early in the morning crowds assemble there with the noise of trumpets and kettle-drums. See those wild fierce men adorned with flowers. They go towards the temple. A blacksmith is ready. Lo! one puts out his tongue, and the blacksmith cuts it: that is to please Kalee: another chooses rather to have an iron bar run through his tongue. Some thrust iron bars and burning coals into their sides. The boldest mount a wooden scaffold and throw themselves down upon iron spikes beneath, stuck in bags of sand. It is very painful to fall upon these spikes; but there is another way of torture quite as painful—it is the swing. Those who determine to swing, allow the blacksmith to drive hooks into the flesh upon their backs, and hanging by these hooks they swing in the air for ten minutes, or even for half an hour. And why all these cruel tortures? To please Kalee, and to make the people wonder and admire, for the multitude around shout with joy as they behold these horrible deeds.

THE CASTES.—The Hindoos pretend that when Brahma created men, he made some out of his mouth, some out of his arms, some out of his breast, and some out of his foot. They say the priests came out of Brahma's mouth, the soldiers came out of his arm, the merchants came out of his breast, the laborers came out of his foot. You may easily guess who invented this history. It was the priests themselves: it was they who wrote the sacred books where this history is found.

The priests are very proud of their high birth, and they call themselves Brahmins.

The laborers, who are told they come out of Brahma's foot, are much ashamed of their low birth. They are called sudras.

You would be astonished to hear the great respect the sudras pay to the high and haughty Brahmins. When a sudra meets a Brahmin in the street, he touches the ground three times with his forehead, then, taking the priest's foot in his hand, he kisses his toe.

The water in which a Brahmin has washed his feet is thought very holy. It is even believed that such water can cure diseases.

A Hindoo prince, who was very ill of a fever, was advised to try this remedy. He invited the Brahmins from all parts of the country to assemble at his palace. Many thousands came. Each, as he arrived, was requested to wash his feet in a basin. This was the medicine given to the sick prince to drink. It cost a great deal of money to procure it; for several shillings were given to each Brahmin to pay him for his trouble, and a good dinner was provided for all. It is said that the prince recovered immediately, but we are quite certain that it was not the water which cured him.

In the holy books, or shasters, great blessings are promised to those who are kind to a Brahmin. Any one who gives him an umbrella will never more be scorched by the sun; any one who gives him a pair of shoes will never have blistered feet; any one who gives him sweet spices will never more be annoyed by ill smells; and any one who gives him a cow will go to heaven.

You may be sure that, after such promises, the Brahmins get plenty of presents; indeed, they may generally be known by their well-fed appearance, as well as by their proud manner of walking. They always wear a white cord hung round their necks.

But we must not suppose that all Brahmins are rich, and all sudras poor; for it is not so. There are so many Brahmins that some can find no employment as priests, and they are obliged to learn trades. Many of them become cooks.

There are sudras as rich as princes; but still a sudra can never be as honorable as a Brahmin, though the Brahmin be the cook and the sudra the master.

But the sudras are not the *most* despised people. Far from it. It is those who have no caste at all who are the most despised. They are called pariahs. These are people who have lost their caste. It is a very easy thing to lose caste, and once lost it can never be regained. A Brahmin would lose his caste by eating with a sudra; a sudra would lose his by eating with a pariah, and by eating with *you*—yes, with *you*, for the Hindoos think that no one is holy but themselves. It often makes a missionary smile when he enters a cottage to see the people putting away their food with haste, lest he should defile it by his touch.

Once an English officer, walking along the road, passed very near a Hindoo just going to eat his dinner; suddenly he saw the man take up the dish and dash it angrily to the ground. Why? The officer's shadow had passed over the food and polluted it.

If you were to invite poor Hindoos to come to a feast, they would not eat if you sat down with them: nor would they eat unless they knew a Hindoo had cooked their food. Even children at school will not eat with children of a lower caste,—or with their teachers, if the teachers are not Hindoos.

There was once a little Hindoo girl named Rajee. She went to a missionary's school, but she would not eat with her schoolfellows, because she belonged to a higher caste than they did. As she lived at the school, her mother brought her food every day, and Rajee sat under a tree to eat it. At the end of two years she told her mother that she wished to turn from idols, and serve the living God. Her mother was much troubled at hearing this, and begged her child not to bring disgrace on the family by becoming a Christian. But Rajee was anxious to save her precious soul. She cared no longer for her caste, for she knew that all she had been taught about it was deceit and folly; therefore one day she sat down and ate with her schoolfellows. When her mother heard of Rajee's conduct, she ran to the school in a rage, and seizing her little daughter by the hair of the head, began to beat her severely. Then she hastened to the priests to ask them whether the child had lost her caste forever. The priests replied, "Has the child got her new teeth?" "No," said the mother. "Then we can cleanse her, and when her new teeth come she will be as pure as ever. But you must pay a good deal of money for the cleansing." Were they not *cunning* priests? and *covetous* priests too?

The money was paid, and Rajee was brought home against her will. Dreadful sufferings awaited the poor child. The cleansing was a cruel business. The priests burned the child's tongue. This was one of their cruelties. When little Rajee was suffered to go back to school, she was so ill that she could not rise from her bed.

The poor deceived mother came to see her. "I am going to Jesus," said the young martyr. The mother began to weep, "O Rajee, we will not let you die."

"But I am glad," the little sufferer replied, "because I shall go to Jesus. If you, mother, would love him, and give up your idols, we should meet again in heaven."

An hour afterwards Rajee went to heaven; but I have never heard whether her mother gave up her idols.

THE GANGES.—This beautiful river waters the sultry plain of Bengal. God made this river to be a blessing, but man has turned it into a curse. The Hindoos say the River Ganges is the goddess Gunga; and they flock from all parts of India to worship her. When they reach the river they bathe in it, and fancy they have washed away all their sins. They carry away large bottles of the sacred water for their friends at home.

But this is not all; very cruel deeds are committed by the side of the river. It is supposed that all who die there will go to the Hindoo heaven. It is therefore the custom to drag dying people out of their beds, and to lay them in the mud, exposed to the heat of the broiling sun, and then to pour pails of water over their heads.

One sick man, who was being carried to the water, covered up as if he were dead, suddenly threw off the covering, and called out, "I am not dead, I am only very ill." He knew that the cruel people who were carrying him were going to cast him into the water while he was still alive: but nothing he could say could save him: the cruel creatures answered, "You may as well die *now* as at any other time;" and so they drowned him, pretending all the while to be very kind.

It is thought a good thing to be thrown into the river after death. The Ganges is the great burying-place; and dead bodies may be seen floating on its waters, while crows and vultures are tearing the flesh from the bones. There would be many more of these horrible sights were it not that many bodies are burned, and their ashes only cast into the river.

Some foolish deceived creatures drown themselves in the Ganges, hoping to be very happy hereafter as a reward. The Brahmins are ready to accompany such people into the water. Some men were once seen going into the river with a large empty jar fastened to the back of each. The empty jar prevented them from sinking; but there was a cup in the hands of each of the poor men, and with these cups they filled the jars, and then they began to sink. One of them grew frightened, and tried to get on shore; but the wicked Brahmins in their boats hunted him, and tried to keep him in the water; however, they could not catch him, and the miserable man escaped. There are villages near the river whither such poor creatures flee, and where they end their days together; for their old friends would not speak to them if they were to return to their homes.

BEGGARS.—As you walk about Hindostan, you will sometimes meet a horrible object, with no other covering than a tiger's skin, or else an orange scarf; his body besmeared with ashes, his hair matted like the shaggy coat of a wild beast, and his nails like birds' claws. The man is a beggar, and a very bold one, because he is considered as one of the holiest of men. Who is he?

A sunnyasee. Who is *he*?

A Brahmin, who wishing to be more holy than other Brahmins (holy as they are), has left all and become a beggar. As a reward, he expects, when he dies, to go straight to heaven, without being first born again in the world. It is wonderful to see the tortures which a sunnyasee will endure. He will stand for years on one leg, till it is full of wounds, or, if he prefers it, he will clench his fist till the nails grow through the hands.

These holy beggars are found in all parts of India, but they are particularly fond of the most desolate spots. Near the mouth of the Ganges there are some desert places, the resort of tigers, and there many of the sunnyasees live in huts. They pretend not to be afraid of the tigers, and the Hindoos think that tigers will not touch such holy men; but it is certain that tigers have been seen dragging some of these proud men into the woods.

There is another kind of beggars called fakirs; they are just as wicked and foolish as the sunnyasees; but they are Mahomedans and not Brahmins.

Animals.—Some of the fiercest and most disagreeable animals are highly honored in India.

The monkey is counted as a god; the consequence is, that the monkeys, finding they are treated with respect, grow very bold, and are continually scrambling upon the roofs of the houses. In one place there is a garden where monkeys riot about at their pleasure, for all in that garden is for them alone, the delicious fruits, the cool fountains, the shady bowers, all are for the worthless, mischievous monkeys.

But if it be strange for men to worship *monkeys*, is it not stranger still to worship *snakes* and *serpents*? Yet there is a temple in India where serpents crawl about at their pleasure, where they are waited upon by priests, and fed with fruits and every dainty. How much delighted must the old serpent be with this worship!

Kites also, those fierce birds, are worshipped. There is meat sold in shops on purpose for them; and it is bought and thrown up in the air to the great greedy creatures.

There are splendid peacocks flying about in the woods, but the Hindoos do not worship them; they shoot and eat them.

Of all the animals in India there is none which terrifies man so much as the tiger. The Bengal tiger is a fine and fierce beast. Woe to the man or woman on whom he springs! What then do you think must become of the man who falls into his den? These dens are generally hid in jungles, which are places covered with trees, and overgrown with shrubs and tall grass.

A gentleman was once walking through a jungle, when he felt himself sinking into the ground, while a cloud of dust blinded his eyes. Soon he heard a low growling noise. He fancied that he had sunk into a den, and so he had. Beside him lay some little tigers, too young indeed to hurt him; but these tigers had a mother, and she could not be far off, though she was not in the den when the stranger fell in. The astonished man felt there was no time to be lost, for the tigress, he knew, would soon return to her cubs. How could he prepare to meet her? He had neither gun nor sword, nor even stick in his hand. But a thought came into his head. Snatching a silk handkerchief from his neck, and taking another from his pocket, he bound them tightly round his arm up to his elbow; and thus prepared to meet his enemy. She soon appeared, crouching on the ground, and then with a spring leaped upon the stranger. At the same moment the brave man thrust his arm between her open jaws, and seizing hold of her rough tongue, twisted it backwards and forwards with all his might. The beast was now unable to close her mouth, and to bite with her sharp fangs; but she could scratch with her sharp claws; and scratch she did, till the clothes were torn off the man's body, and the flesh from his bones. But the brave man would not loose his hold;

and the tigress was tired out first: alarmed,—with a sudden start backward, she jerked her tongue out of the man's hand, and rushed out of the den and out of the jungle.

How glad was the man to escape from a horrible fate! his body was faint and bleeding; but his life was preserved, and his heart overflowed with gratitude to God for his wonderful deliverance. He who delivered Daniel from the lion's den delivered him from the tiger's den. The tiger's mouth, indeed, had not been shut; but his open mouth had not been suffered to devour the Lord's servant.

THE THUGS.

There is a set of people in India more dangerous than wild beasts. They are called Thugs, that is, deceivers; and well do they deserve the name; for their whole employment is to *deceive* that they may *destroy*. Yet they are not ashamed of their wickedness; for they worship the goddess Kalee, and they know that she delights in blood. Before they set out on one of their cruel journeys, they bow down before the image of Kalee, and they ask her to bless the shovel and the cloth that they hold in their hands.

What are they for?

The cloth is to strangle poor travellers, and the shovel to dig their graves.

A Hindoo family were once travelling when they overtook three men on the way. These men seemed very civil and obliging; and they soon got acquainted with the family, and accompanied them on their journey. Who were these men? Alas! they were Thugs. It was very foolish of the family to be so ready to go with strangers. At last they came up to three other men, who were sitting under the shade of a tree, eating sugared rice. These men also were Thugs; and they had agreed with the other Thugs to help them in their wicked plans. But the family thought they were kind and friendly men, and consented to sit down with them in the shade, and to partake of their food. They did not know that with the rice was mixed a sort of drug to cause people to fall asleep. The family ate and fell asleep: and when they were asleep, the Thugs strangled them all with their cloths,—the father, the mother, and the five young people,—and then with their shovels they dug their graves. But before they buried them they stripped them of their garments and their jewels; for it was to get their precious spoils they had committed these dreadful murders. The Thugs went afterwards to the priests of Kalee to receive a blessing, and they rewarded the priests by giving them some of their stolen treasures.

But, after all, these wicked men did not escape punishment; for the English governors heard of their crimes, and caught them, and brought them to justice. Then these murderers confessed the wicked deed just related: but this was not their only crime; for it had been the business of their lives to rob and to destroy.

Do not these Thugs resemble him who is always walking about seeking whom he may devour? Only he destroys the *soul* as well as the *body*. He is the great Deceiver, and the great Destroyer. None but God can keep us from falling into his power: therefore we pray, "Deliver us from evil," or from the evil one.

THE HINDOO WOMEN.

It is a miserable thing to be a Hindoo lady. While she is a very little girl, she is allowed to play about, but when she comes to be ten or twelve years old, she is shut up in the back rooms of the house till she is married; and when she is married she is shut up still. She may indeed walk in the garden at the back of the house, but nowhere else.

Hindoo ladies are not taught even those trifling accomplishments which Chinese ladies learn: they can neither paint, nor play music; much less can they read and write. They amuse themselves by putting on their ornaments, or by making curries and sweetmeats to please their husbands: but most of their time they spend in idleness, sauntering about and chattering nonsense. As rich Hindoos have several wives, the ladies are not alone; and being so much together, they quarrel a great deal.

Some English ladies once visited the house of a rich Hindoo. They were led into the court at the back of the house, and shown into a little chamber. One by one some women came in, all looking very shy and afraid to speak; yet dressed very fine in muslin sarees, worked with gold and silver flowers, and they were adorned with pearls and diamonds. At last they ventured to admire the clothes of their visitors, and even to touch them. Then they asked the English ladies to come and see their jewels; and they took them into a little dark chamber with gratings for windows, and displayed their treasures. They talked very loud, and all together and so foolishly, that the ladies reproved them. The poor creatures replied, "We should like to learn to read and work like the English ladies; but we have nothing to do, and so we are accustomed to be idle, and to talk foolishly. Do come again, and bring us books, and pictures, and dolls."

You see what useless, wearisome lives the Hindoo *ladies* lead. Now hear what hard and wretched lives the *poor* women lead. The wife of a poor man rises from her mat before it is day, and by the light of a lamp spins cotton for the family clothing. Next she feeds the children, and sweeps the house and yard, and cleans the brass and stone vessels. Then she washes the rice, bruises, and boils it. By this time it is ten o'clock, when she goes with some other women to bathe in the river, or if there be no river near, in a great tank of rain-water. While there, she often makes a clay image of her god, and worships it with prayers, and bowings, and offerings of fruit and flowers, for nearly an hour. On her return home she prepares the curry for dinner: her kitchen is a clay furnace in the yard, and there she boils the rice. When dinner is ready, she dares not sit down with her husband to eat it: no, she places it respectfully before his mat, and then retires to the yard. Her little boys eat with their father; but her little girls dine with her upon the food that is left.

It is not the busy life she leads that makes a poor woman unhappy: it is the ill-treatment she endures. A kind word is seldom spoken to her: but a hard blow is often given. Her own boys are encouraged to insult her because she is only a woman. She is taught to worship her husband as a god, however bad he may be. There is a proverb which shows how much women are despised in India. "How can you place the black rice-pot beside the golden spice-box!" By the rice-box a woman is meant: by the spice-box a man: and the meaning of the proverb is that a wife is unworthy to sit at the same table with her husband.

In this manner a *wife* is treated: a *widow* is still more despised. However young she may be, she is not allowed to marry again; but is obliged to live in her father's house, or (if she has no father) in her brother's house, to do the hardest work, and never to eat more than one meal a day, and that meal of the coarsest food. Widows used to burn themselves in a great fire with their husbands' dead bodies; but the English government has forbidden them to do so any more; but their hard-hearted relations make them as miserable as possible.

Missionaries.—There are hundreds of missionaries in India; but not nearly enough for so many millions of people. The Hindoos call them Padri-Sahibs, which means "Father-Gentlemen," and they give them this name to show their love, as well as respect.

Once a missionary who had been long in India was

going back to England for a little while. It was from Calcutta that he set sail. The Christian Hindoos stood in crowds by the river-side to bid him farewell. Among the rest was a little girl with her parents. She was a gracious child, who had turned from idols to serve the living God. The missionary said to her, "Well, my child, you know I am going to England. What shall I bring you from that country?"

"I do not want anything," she modestly replied. "I have my parents, and my brother, and the Padri-Sahibs, and my books, what can I want more?"

"But," said the missionary, "you are only a little girl, and surely you would like something from England. Shall I bring you some playthings?"

"No, thank you," said the child; "I do not want playthings—I am learning to read."

"Come, come," said the missionary, "shall I bring you a playfellow, a white child from England!"

"No, no," answered the little girl, "it would be taking her from her parents."

"Well then," said her friend, "is there nothing I can bring you?"

"Well, if you are so kind as to insist on bringing me something, ask the Christians in England to send me a Bible-book and more PADRI-SAHIBS."

This was a good request indeed, but to get Padri-

MISSIONARY'S HOUSE. p. 128.

Sahibs is a hard thing to do. Who can tell how much good they have done already! There are many Christian villages in India, and they are as different from heathen villages as a dove's nest is different from a tiger's den.

Some very wicked men have been converted. You have heard of those proud and hateful beggars, the Sunnyasees and the Fakirs.

One day a missionary, who had gone for his health to the Himalaya Mountains, was walking in the verandah of his house, when he was surprised by a man suddenly throwing himself down at his feet, and embracing his knees. The missionaary could not tell who this man was, for a dark blanket covered the man's head and face.. But soon the covering was lifted up, and a swarthy and withered countenance was shown; the missionary knew it to be that of an old Fakir he once had known, as the chief priest of a gang of robbers, but now the Mahomedan was become a Christian; and he had travelled six hundred miles, hoping to see once more the face of his teacher; and lo! he had seen it at last.

SCHOOLS.—The Hindoos have schools of their own, but only for boys. The scholars sit in a shed, cross-legged upon mats, and learn to scratch letters with iron pins upon large leaves. But what can they learn from Brahmin teachers but foolish tales about false gods?

Missionaries have far better schools, where the Bible is taught; and missionaries' wives have schools for girls; and sometimes they take pity on poor orphans, and receive them into their houses.

One evening as a Christian lady was returning home, she saw a Hindoo woman lying on the ground, and a little boy sitting by her side. The lady spoke kindly to the sick woman, and then the little boy looked up and said, with tears in his eyes, "My mother is sick, and has nothing to eat; I fear she will die." The lady had compassion on the mother and the child, and hastening home, she sent her servant to fetch them both. They were soon put to rest on a nice clean mat, with a blanket to cover them; but the mother died next morning. The little boy was left an orphan, but not forlorn, nor friendless, for the Christian lady took care of him. He was five years old, thin and delicate, and much fairer than most Hindoo children. He had many winning ways; but he had a proud heart. He was proud of his name, "Ramchunda," because it was the name of a great false god: but when he had learned about the true God, he asked for a new name, and was called "John." His wishing to change his name was a good sign: and there were other good signs in this little orphan; and before he died,—for he died soon,—he showed plainly that he had not a new *name* only, but a new *nature.*

Little Phebe was another child received by a missionary's wife. She was not an orphan, yet she was as much to be pitied as an orphan; for her mother told the missionaries that if they did not take the child, she would throw her to the jackals. It was a happy exchange for the infant to leave so cruel a mother to be reared by a Christian lady, who, instead of throwing her to jackals, brought her to Jesus.

She died when only five years old by an accident: when washing her hands in the great tank she fell in, and was drowned.

But some Hindoo children, though carefully instructed, do not grow gentle and loving, like John and Phebe.

The tents of some English soldiers were pitched in a lonely part of India; and the night was dark, when an officer's lady thought she heard the sound of a child crying. The lady sent her servants out to look, and at last they brought in a little girl of four years old. And where do you think they had found her? Buried up to her throat in a bog, her little head alone peeping out. And who do you think had put her there? Her cruel mother. Yes, she had left her there to die.

This child gave a great deal of trouble to the kind lady who had saved her, nor did she show her any love in return for her kindness; and after keeping her about two years, the lady sent her to a missionary's school.

You see how cruelly mothers in India sometimes treat their children. Their religion teaches them to be cruel.

A mother is taught to believe that if her babe is sick, an evil spirit is angry. To please this evil spirit, she will put her babe in a basket, and hang it up in a tree for three days. She goes then to look at it, and if it be alive, she takes it home. But how seldom does she find it alive! Either the ants or the vultures have eaten it, or it is starved to death.

When there is a famine in the land, many mothers will sell their children for sixpence each: and if they cannot sell them, they will leave them to perish.

One missionary received fifty-one poor starving children into his house: they were always crying, "Sahib, roti, roti;" that is, "Master, bread, bread." But the bread came to late too save their lives; for all died except one.

Yet these sick children were very wicked.

One of them stole a brass basin, and sold it for sweetmeats. Though very kindly treated, some of them wished to escape; and to prevent it, the missionary tied them together in strings of fifteen.

There is a tribe in India called Khunds; and they sprinkle their fields with children's blood, and they say this is the way to make the corn grow. The English government once rescued eighty poor children from the Khunds, and sent them to a Christian school. What miserable little creatures they were when they arrived! but they were soon clothed and comforted; and taught to hold a needle, and to know their letters; and, better still, to pronounce the name of Jesus. Like these poor little captives, we were all condemned to die, till Jesus rescued us, and promised everlasting life to those who believe.

THE ENGLISH IN INDIA.

There are many rich English gentlemen living in India: some are judges, and some are merchants, and some are officers in the army. They dwell in large and grand houses, with many windows down to the ground, and a wide verandah to keep off the sun. Instead of *glass*, there is *grass* in the windows: the blinds are made of sweet-scented grass, and servants outside continually pour water on the grass to make the air cool. Instead of *fires*, they have *fans*. These fans are like large screens hanging from the ceiling, and waving to and fro to refresh the company. Instead of carpets there are mats on the loor; and round the beds gauze curtains are drawn to keep out the insects.

The servants are all Hindoos, and a great number are kept; and this is necessary, because each servant will only do one kind of work.

Each horse has two servants, one to take care of it, and the other to cut grass: even the dog has a boy to look after it alone. The servants do not live in their master's house, but in small huts near. The place where they live is called "the compound."

When English people travel they do not go in carriages, but in palanquins. A palanquin is like a child's cot, only larger; and there a traveller can sleep at his ease.

The Even who carry the palanquins are called "Bearers." The nurses are called Ayahs. Babies are carried out of doors by their ayahs, but children of three or four are taken out by the bearers.

There was once a little girl of three years old who taught her bearer to fear God.

Little Mary was walking out in a grove with her heathen bearer. She observed him stop at a small Hindoo temple, and bow down to the stone image before the door.

The lisping child inquired,—"Saamy, what for, you do that?"

"O, missy," said he, "that is my god!"

"Your god!" exclaimed the child, "your god, Saamy! Why your god can no see, no can hear, no can walk—your god stone! My God make you, make me, make everything!" Yet Saamy still, whenever he passed the temple, bowed down to his idol: and still the child reproved him. Though the old man would not mind, yet he loved his baby teacher. Once when he thought she was going to England he said to her,—"What will poor Saamy do when missy go to England? Saamy no father, no mother."

"O Saamy!" replied the child, "if you love God he will be your father, and mother too."

The poor bearer promised with tears in his eyes that he would love God. "Then," said she, "you must learn my prayers;" and she began to teach him the Lord's Prayer. Soon afterwards Mary's papa was surprised to see the bearer enter the room at the time of family prayers, and still more surprised to see him take off his turban, kneel down, and repeat the Lord's

Prayer after his master. The lispings of the babe had brought the old man to God: Saamy did not only bow the knee, he worshipped in spirit and in truth, and became a real Christian.

CHIEF CITIES.

There are three great cities which may be called English cities, though in India: because Englishmen built them, and live in them, and rule over them. Their names are Calcutta, Madras, and Bombay.

The capital city is Calcutta. There the chief governor resides. Part of Calcutta is called the Black Town, and it is only a heap of mud huts crowded with Hindoos. The other part of Calcutta is called the English town; and it consists of beautiful houses by the river-side, each house surrounded by a charming garden and a thick grove.

Madras is built on a plain by the sea, and is adorned by fine avenues of trees, amongst which the English live in elegant villas and gardens. Here also there is a Black town. It is very hard to land at Madras, because there is no harbor.

Bombay has one of the best harbors in the world. It is built on a small island covered with cocoa-nut groves.

Now let us compare these places with each other.

Calcutta boasts of her fine river, but then the ground is flat and marshy; and therefore the air is damp and unhealthy, and there are no grand prospects.

Madras is very dry, and sandy, and dusty; but then there is the sea to enliven and refresh it.

Bombay has the sea also, besides the groves, and at a little distance, high mountains, which look beautiful, and which it is delightful to visit. There are no such mountains near Calcutta or Madras.

These are the chief English cities. I must now speak of the favorite city of the Hindoos.

It is Benares on the Ganges.

You might go from Calcutta in a boat, and after sailing four hundred miles, you would reach Benares. The Hindoos say that it was built by their god Sheeva, of gold and precious stones; but that, as we are living in a bad time, it *appears* to be made of bricks and mud, though really very different. They say that Benares is eighty thousand steps nearer heaven than any other city, and that whoever dies there (even though he eat BEEF!) will go to heaven.

A missionary once reproved a Hindoo for telling lies. The answer was, "Why, what of that? do I not live at Benares?" The man thought he was quite safe, however wicked he might be.

In walking about Benares a stranger might be surprised to meet every now and then a white bull, with a hump on its back, without a driver or a rider, or any one to keep it in order. You must know that a white bull is said to belong to the chief god of Benares, and it is considered a sacred animal, and is allowed to do as it pleases.

And how does it behave?

It behaves much in the same manner as a child would who had its own way. The white bull helps itself to the fruit and vegetables sold in the streets, and even to the sweetmeats. It has a great taste for flowers; and it cunningly hides itself near the doors of the temples, to watch for the people coming out with their garlands of marigolds round their necks. At these the bull eagerly snatches with its tongue, and swallows them in a moment. Finding it is petted by every one, it grows so bold, as to walk into the houses, and even to go up the stone stairs on to the roof, where it seems to enjoy the cool air, as it quietly chews the cud.

In the spring the white bulls like to wander out in the fields to eat the tender green grass. A farmer finding one of these bulls in his fields, made him get into a boat, and sent him by a man across the river Ganges. But the cunning creature came back in the evening; for he watched till he saw some people setting out in a boat, and then jumped in; and though the passengers tried to turn him out, he would stay there. In this way he got back to the cornfields.

So much respected are these bulls that a Hindoo would sooner lose his own life than suffer one of them to be killed. An English gentleman was just going to shoot one that had broken into his garden, when his Hindoo servant rushed between him and the bull, saying, "Shoot me, sir, shoot me, but let him go." You may be sure that the gentleman did not shoot the servant, and I think it probable he spared the bull's life.

There is one more city to be noticed.

DELHI was once the grandest city in India, and the seat of the great Moguls, those Mahomedans who conquered India before the British came. The ancient palace is still to be seen: it is built of red stone; but its ornaments are gone; where is now the room lined with crystal, the golden palm-tree with diamond fruits, and the golden peacock with emerald wings, overshadowing the monarch's throne?

The Persians have stripped the palace of all its gorgeous splendor.

We have now described the two most numerous nations in the world, China and Hindostan. They contain together more than half the world. In some respects they are alike, and in some respects they are different. In these respects they are different.

IN CHINA.	IN HINDOSTAN.
There is one emperor.	There is no emperor, and the English govern the country.
There is one language.	There are many.
They use chairs, and tables, and beds.	They sit and sleep on mats.
They eat with chop-sticks.	They eat with their fingers.
They wear shoes.	They go barefoot, and wear sandals.
The men shave their heads except one lock.	The men twist up their hair with a comb.
They seldom wash themselves.	They bathe often.
They eat pigs more than any other meat.	They abhor pigs.
They are grave and silent.	They are merry and talkative.
They are industrious.	They are idle.
The most learned rise to be great men.	Every one is high and low according to his caste.
They mind the laws.	They care not for laws.
The land is well cultivated.	There is much waste land, and many jungles.

Now let us consider in what respects they are *alike*.

China and Hindostan are alike in these respects. They are both very *populous*, though China has twice as many inhabitants as Hindostan.

In both rice is the chief food.

In both large grown-up families live together.

In both the women are shut up.

In both foreigners are hated.

In both conjurers are admired.

In both many idols are worshipped.

In both there are ancient sacred books.

In both the people are deceitful, unmerciful to the poor, and in the habit of destroying their own little girls when babies.

In both it is believed that the soul after death goes into another body, and is born over and over again into this world.

Is it not mournful to think that more than half the people in the world have no bright hope to cheer a dying bed? One poor Hindoo was heard to exclaim as he was dying, "Where shall I go *last* of all?" He asked a wise question. He wanted to know where, after having been born ever so many times, he should be put for *ever* and *ever*. That is the great point we all want to know. But the Hindoo and the Chinaman cannot know this: they have never heard of *everlasting* happiness.

Circassia.

THIS is not a vast country like China, or Hindostan. It may be called a nook, it is so small compared with some great kingdoms: but it is famous on account of the beauty of the people. They are fair, like Europeans, with handsome features, and fine figures. But their beauty has done them harm, and not good; for the cruel Turks purchase many of the Circassian women, because they are beautiful, and shut them up in their houses. Perhaps you will be surprised to hear that the young Circassians think it a fine thing to go to Turkey—to live in fine palaces and gardens, instead of remaining in their own simple cottages. But I think that when they find themselves confined between high walls, they must sigh to think of their flocks and their farms at home, and more than all, of the dear relations they have left behind.

Circassia is a pleasant country, situated near the noble mountains of Caucasus. The snow on the mountains cools the air, and makes Circassia as pleas ant to live in as our own England. Indeed, if you were suddenly to be transported into Circassia, you would be ready to exclaim, "Is not this England? Here are apple-trees, and pear-trees, and plum-trees, like those in my father's garden: those sounds are like the notes of the blackbird and thrush, which sing among the hawthorns in English woods."

But look again, you will see vines interlacing their fruitful branches among the spreading oaks. You do not see such vines in England. But hark! what do I hear? It is a sound never heard in England. It is the yell of jackals.

Manners of the People.—There is no country in the world where the people are as kind to strangers as in Circassia. Every family, however poor, has a guest-house. There is the family-house, with its orchard, and stables, and at a little distance, another house for strangers. This is no more than a large room, with a stable at one end. The walls are made of wicker-work, plastered with clay. There is no ceiling but the rafters, and no floor but the bare earth. Yet there is a wide chimney, where a blazing fire is kept up with a pile of logs. And there is a sofa or divan, covered with striped silk, and many neat mats to serve as beds for as many travellers as may arrive. The wind may whistle through the chinks, and the rain come through the roof, but the stranger is well warmed, and comfortably lodged; and above all, he has the host to wait upon him with more attention than a servant. The supper is served as soon as the sun sets.

But where is the table? There is none. Is the supper placed on the floor? Not so. It is brought in on stools with three legs. They answer the purpose of tables, trays, and dishes, all in one. What is the fare served up? This is the sort of dinner provided. On the first table is placed a flat loaf; the gravy in the middle, and the meat all round. When this is taken away, another table is brought in with cheese-cakes; a third with butter and honey; a fourth with a pie; a fifth with a cream; and last of all, a table, with a wooden bowl of curdled milk. The company have no plates; but each Circassian carries a spoon and a knife in his girdle, and with these he helps himself. The servants who stand by, are not forgotten: a piece of meat or of pie-crust is often given to one of them; it is curious to see the men take it into a corner to eat it there. There are many hungry poor waiting at the door of the guest-house, ready to help the servants to devour the remains of the feast; and there is often a great deal of food left; for there are generally *ten* tables, and sometimes there are *forty* tables. The guests are expected to taste the food on each, however many there may be.

Instead of wine, there is a drink called shuat handed to the guests: it is distilled from grain and honey. Vegetables are not much eaten in Circassia: for greens are considered fit only for beasts: and there are no potatoes. Pies, and tarts, and tartlets of various kinds are too well liked, and the finest ladies in the land are skilful in making them.

The family live in a thatched cottage, called "the family-house." It is not divided into rooms. If a man wants several rooms, he builds several houses.

As you approach the dwelling of a Circassian, you hear the barking of dogs, and upon coming nearer, you see women milking cows, and feeding poultry, and boys tending goats, and leading horses.

If you go into the farm-yard, you will see among the animals, the buffalo—but no pig. There are, however, wild boars in the woods.

Circassian Women.—They are not shut up as Hindoo, and Chinese, and Turkish ladies are. They do not indeed go into the guest-house to see strangers; but strangers are sometimes invited into the family-house to see them.

An Englishman, who visited a family-house, was introduced to the wife and daughter. They both rose up when he entered: nor would they sit down, till he sat down; and this respect ladies show not only to gentlemen, but even to the poorest peasants. The only furniture in the house was the divan, on which the ladies sat; a pile of boxes, containing the beds, which were to be spread on the floor at night; and a loom for weaving cloth, and spindles for spinning.

The daughter, who was sixteen, was dressed in a skirt of striped silk, with a blue bodice, and silver clasps; and she wore a cap of scarlet cloth, adorned with silver lace—her light hair flowing over her shoulders: yet though so finely arrayed, her feet were bare; for she only put on her red slippers when she walked out. The mother was covered with a loose calico wrapper, and her face was concealed by a thick white veil. The visitor laid some needle-cases at the ladies' feet, for it is not the custom for them to receive presents in their hands.

The needle-cases greatly delighted the young Hafiza and her mother. The present was well chosen, because the Circassian women are very industrious, supplying their husbands and brothers with all their clothes, from the woollen bonnet to the morocco shoe. The wool, the flax, and the hemp, are all prepared at home by the mothers, and made into clothes by the girls, who first spin the thread, then weave the cloth, and finish by sewing the seams. Some girls are very clever in knitting silver lace for trimming garments. A girl named Dussepli was famous for her skill in this art, indeed her name signifies, "Shining as lace."

An Englishman went to the place where she lived to buy some of her lace. He was shown into the guest-house, and he soon saw Dussepli approaching in a pair of high pattens. At first sight there was nothing pleasing in Dussepli, but when she spoke she seemed so kind, and so true, that it was impossible not to like her. By her industry in knitting lace, and dyeing cloth, she helped to support her father, who was poor.

THE CIRCASSIAN MEN.—War is their chief occupation. Working in the fields is left to the women, and the little boys, and the slaves. There is, alas! great occasion for the men to fight, as the land has long been infested with many dangerous enemies.

The Russians are endeavoring to conquer the Circassians: but the Circassians declare they will die sooner than yield. Long ago the enemies must have triumphed, had it not been for the high mountains which afford hiding-places for the poor hunted inhabitants. Every man carries a gun, a pistol, a dagger, and a sword; and the nobles are distinguished by a bow, and a quiver of arrows. The usual dress is of coarse dark cloth, and consists of a tunic, trowsers, and gaiters. The cap or bonnet is of sheepskin, or goatskin.

The boys are taught from their infancy to be hardy and manly. They are brought up in a singular way. Instead of remaining at home, they are given at three years old, into the care of a stranger: and the reason of this custom is, that they may not be petted by their parents. The stranger is called "foster-father," and he teaches any boy under his care to ride well, and to shoot at a mark. The boy follows his foster-father over the mountains, urging his horses to climb tremendous heights, and to rush down ravines; and appeasing his hunger with a mouthful of honey from the bag, fastened to his girdle. Such is the life he leads, till he is a tall and a strong youth; and then he returns home to his parents. His foster-father presents him with a horse, and weapons of war, and requires no payment in return for all his care.

Men brought up in this manner must be wild, bold, restless, and ignorant. Such are the Circassians. They care not for learning, as the Chinese do, but only for bravery. We cannot wonder at this, when we remember what enemies they have in their land. The Russians have built many strong towers, whence they shoot at all who come near. But, not satisfied

Guz Beg, the "Lion of Circassia." p. 149.

with this, they often come forth and rob the villages.

There was a Circassian, (and he may be still alive,) called Gus Beg; and he gained for himself the name of the "Lion of Circassia." He was always leading out little bands of men to attack the Russians. One day he found some Russian soldiers reaping in the fields, and when he came near they ran away in terror, leaving two hundred scythes in the field, which he seized. But a great calamity befel this Lion. He had an only son. When he first led the boy to the wars, he charged him never to shrink from the enemy, but to cut his way through the very midst. One day Guz Beg had ridden into the thick of the Russian soldiers, when suddenly a ball pierced his horse, and he was thrown headlong on the ground. There lay the Lion among the hunters. In another moment he would have been killed, when suddenly a youthful warrior flew to his rescue;—it was his own son. But what could *one* do among so *many!* A troop of Circassian horse rushed to the spot, and bore away Guz Beg; but they were too late to save his son. They bore away the *body* only of the brave boy. Guz Beg was deeply grieved; but he continued still to fight for his country.

See those black heaps of ashes. In that spot there

once lived a prince named Zefri Bey, with his four hundred servants; but his dwellings were burned to the ground by the Russians. That prince fled to Turkey to plead for help. What would have become of his wife, and little girls, if a kind friend had not taken them under his care? This friend was hump-backed, but very brave. Some English travellers went to visit him, and were received in the guest-house and regaled with a supper of many tables. Next day the little girls came to the guest-house and kissed their hands. The daughter of the hump-backed man accompanied them. The children were delighted with some toys the traveller gave them, and the kind young lady accepted needles and scissors. But where was the wife of Zefri Bey? A servant was sent to inquire after her, and found her in rags, lying on a mat, without even a counterpane, and weeping bitterly. Had no one given her clothes, and coverings? Yes, but she gave everything away, for she had been used, as a princess, to make presents, and now she cared for nothing. Such are the miseries which the Russians bring upon Circassia.

THE GOVERNMENT.—There is no king of Circassia; but there are many princes.

The people pay great respect to these princes, standing in their presence, and giving them the first place at feasts, and in the battle-field. But though the people honor them, they do not obey them.

There is a parliament in Circassia, but it does not meet in a house, but in a grove. Every man who pleases may come, but only old men may speak. If a young man were to give his opinions, no attention would be paid. The warriors sit on the grass, and hang up their weapons of war on the boughs above their heads, while they fasten their horses to the stems of the trees.

The speakers are gentle in their tones of voice and behavior. The Circassians admire sweet winning speeches. They say there are three things which mark a great man; a sharp sword, a sweet tongue, and forty tables. What do they mean by these? By a sharp sword they mean bravery, by a sweet tongue they mean soft speeches, and by forty tables they mean giving plentiful suppers to neighbors and to strangers. Are the Circassians right in this way of thinking? No—for though bravery is good, and speaking well is good, and giving away is good, these are not the greatest virtues: and people may be brave, and speak well, and give away much, and yet be wicked: for they may be without the love of God in their hearts. What are the greatest virtues? These three, Faith, Hope, and Charity. These are graces which come from God.

Servants.—There are slaves in Circassia, called serfs. But they are so well treated, that they are not like the slaves of other countries. They live in huts round their master's dwelling; they work in the fields, and wait upon the guests, and share in the good fare on the little tables.

When a Circassian takes a Russian prisoner, he makes him a slave, and gives him the hardest work to do. Yet the Russians are much happier with their Circassian masters than in their own country.

Once a Circassian said to his Russian slave, "I am going to send you back to Russia." The man fell at his master's feet, saying, "Rather than do so, use me as your dog; beat me, tie me up, and give me your bones to pick." The master then told him that he had not spoken in earnest, and that he would not send him away, and then the poor fellow began to shout, and to jump with joy.

Brotherhoods.—There is a very remarkable plan in Circassia, unlike the plans in other countries. A certain number of men agree to call themselves "brothers." These brothers help each other on every occasion, and visit at each other's houses frequently They are not received in the guest-house, but in the family-house, and are treated by all the family as if they were really the brothers of the master.

A brotherhood sometimes consists of two thousand, but sometimes of only twenty persons.

RELIGION.—Circassia, though beautiful, is an unhappy country. The Russians keep the people in continual fear; this is a great evil. But there is another nation who have done the Circassians still greater harm. I mean the Turks. And what have they done to them? They have persuaded them to turn Mahomedans. The greatest harm that can be done to any one, is to give him a false religion. There are no grand mosques in Circassia, because there are no towns: but in every little village there is a clay cottage, where prayers are offered up in the name of Mahomet. There can be no minaret to such a miserable mosque: so the man who calls the hours of prayer, climbs a tall tree, by the help of notches, and getting into a basket at the top, makes the rocks and hills resound with his cry. I ow different shall be the sound one day heard in every land; when all people shall believe in Jesus. "Then shall the inhabitants of the rocks sing—then shall they shout from the top of the mountains, and give glory unto the *Lord*," and not to Mahomet. (Is. xlii. 11, 12.)

But though the Circassians call themselves Mahomedans, they keep many of their old customs, and these customs show that they once heard about Christ.

It is their custom to dedicate every boy to God: but not really to *God*, for in truth they dedicate him to the *cross*. Let me give you an account of one of the feasts of dedication.

The place of meeting was a green, shaded by spreading oak-trees. In the midst stood a cross. Each family who came to the feast, brought a little table, and placed it before the cross; and on each table, there were loaves, and a sort of bread called "pasta." There was a blazing fire on the green, round which the elder women sat, while the younger preferred the shade of a thicket. The priest took a loaf of bread in one hand, and in the other, a large cup of shuat, (a kind of wine) and holding them out towards the cross, blessed them. While he did this, men, women, and children, knelt around, and bowed their heads to the ground. Afterwards, the shuat and the bread were handed about amongst the company. But this was only the beginning of the feast. Afterwards, a calf, a sheep, and two goats were brought to the cross to be blessed. Then a little of their hair was singed by a taper, and then they were taken away to be slaughtered. Now the merriment began: some moved forward to cut up the animals, and to boil their flesh in large kettles on fires kindled on the green; many young men amused themselves with racing, leaping, and hurling stones, while the elder people sat and talked. When the meat was boiled, it was distributed among the sixty tables, and then the priest blessed the food. And then the feasting began. Does it not seem as if the Circassians must once have learned about Jesus crucified, and about his supper of bread and wine, and about the Jewish feasts and sacrifices? Once, perhaps, they knew the true religion, but they soon forgot it, and though they still remember the *Cross*, they have forgotten *Christ*; and though they still bless the bread and the cup, they know nothing of redeeming love. Do you not long to send missionaries to Circassia? Well, some good Scotch missionaries went there some years ago, but alas! the Russians sent them away. Their thatched cottages may still be seen, and their fruitful orchards, but they themselves are gone. There are, however, a few German Christians in Circassia. They are not missionaries, but only farmers, therefore the Russians allow them to remain. They have a little church, where the Bible is read, and God is worshipped. You will be glad to hear a few Circassians may be seen amongst the congregation; they were converted by the Scotch missionaries, and they have remained faithful amongst their heathen neighbors.

Circassia is situated between two seas:—

The Black Sea, and

The Caspian Sea.

What a wonderful place is the Caspian Sea. It is like a lake, only so immensely large, that it is called a sea. The waters of lakes are fresh, like those of rivers; but the waters of the Caspian are salt, but not so salt as the salt sea. The shores of the Caspian are flat, and unwholesome. You might think as you stood there, that you were by the great ocean, for there are waves breaking on the sands, and water as far as the eye can reach, but there is no freshness in the air as by the real sea.

The mountains of Caucasus run through Circassia. They are quite low compared to the Himalaya; they are about the height of the Alps, and the tops are covered with snow. But the valleys between these mountains, are not like the Swiss valleys, which are broad and pleasant; but these valleys are narrow, and dark, and not fit to live in, yet they are of great use as hiding-places for the Circassians. When pursued by a Russian, a Circassian will urge his horse to dash down the dark valley, and lest his horse should be alarmed by the sight of the dangerous depth below, he will cover the animal's eyes with his cloak. Thus, many a bold rider escapes from a cruel soldier.

Georgia.

WHEN you hear of Circassia, you will generally hear of Georgia too, for the countries lie close together, and resemble one another in many respects. But though so near, their climate is different; for Circassia lies beyond the mountains of Caucasus, and is therefore, exposed to the cold winds of the north. But Georgia lies beneath the mountains, and is sheltered from the chill blasts. Georgia is, therefore, far more fruitful than Circassia, the people, too, are less fair, and less industrious. The sides of the hills are clothed with vines, and houses with deep verandahs are scattered among the vineyards, and women wrapped in long white sheets may be seen reposing in the porticoes, enjoying the soft air, and lovely prospect. While Circassian ladies are busy weaving and milking, the Georgian ladies loll upon their couches, and do nothing. Which do you think are the happier? These Georgian ladies, too, though very handsome, are much disfigured by painted faces, and stained eyebrows. Their countenances, too, are lifeless, and silly, as might be expected, since they waste their time in idleness. Over their foreheads, they wear a kind of low crown, called a tiara.

There is no country where so much wine is drank as in Georgia, even a laborer is allowed five bottles a day. The grapes are exceedingly fine, quite different from the little berries called grapes in Circassia. The casks are very curious, they are the skins of buffaloes, and as the tails and legs are not cut off, a skin filled with wine looks like a dead, or a sleeping buffalo.

And what is the religion of Georgia? It is the Russian religion, because the Russians have conquered the country. They cannot conquer the brave, and active Circassians, but they have conquered the soft, and indolent Georgians. The Georgians are called Christians, but the Greek Church, which is the Russian religion, is a Christianity, laden with ceremonies and false doctrines.

TIFLIS.

There is but one town in Georgia. It is beautifully situated on the steep banks of a river, with terraces of houses, embosomed in vineyards. So little do the people care for reading, that there is not a bookseller's shop in the town, and it is very seldom that a book-case is seen in a house; for the Georgians love show and entertainments, and idleness, but not study.

Tartary.

This is one of the largest countries in the world, yet it does not contain as many people as the small land of France. How is this? You will not be surprised that many people do not live there, when you hear what sort of a country it is.

Fancy a country quite flat, as far as eye can see, except where a few low sand-hills rise; a country quite bare, except where the coarse grass grows;—a country quite dry, except where some narrow muddy streams run. Such is Tartary. What is a country without hills, without trees, without brooks? Can it be pleasant? This flat, bare, dry plain, is called the steppes of Tartary. In one part of Tartary, there is a chain of mountains, and there are a few towns, and trees, but *very few*. You may travel a long while without seeing one.

Nothing can be so dreary as the steppes appear in winter time. The high wind sweeping along the plain, drives the snow into high heaps, and often hurls the poor animals into a cold grave. Sledges cannot be used, because they cannot slide on such uneven ground. But if the *white* ground looks dreary in winter, the *black* ground looks hideous in summer; for the hot sun turns the grass black, and fills the air with black dust, and there are no shady groves, no cool hills, no refreshing brooks. There must, indeed, be a *little* shade among the thistles, as they grow to twice the height of a man; but how different is such shade from the shade of spreading oaks like ours! Instead of nice fruit, there is bitter wormwood growing among the grass, and when the cows eat it, their milk becomes bitter.

WILD ANIMALS.—The most common, is a pretty little creature called the sooslik. It is very much like a squirrel.

But can it live where squirrels live,—in the hollows of trees? Where are the trees in the steppe? The sooslik makes a house for itself by digging a hole in the ground, just as rabbits do in England. Will it not surprise you to hear that wolves follow the same plan, and even the wild dogs? The houses the dogs make are very convenient, for the entrance is very narrow, and there is plenty of room below.

There are some very odious animals on the steppe. Snakes and toads. Yes, showers of toads sometimes fall. But neither snakes nor toads are as great a plague as locusts. These little animals, not bigger than a child's thumb, are more to be dreaded than a troop of wolves. And why? Because they come in such immense numbers. The eggs lie hid in the ground all the winter. O if it were known *where* they were concealed, they would soon be destroyed. But no one knows where they are till they are hatched. In the first warm days of spring the young animals come forth, and immediately they begin crawling on the ground in one immense flock, eating up all the grass as they pass along; in a month they can fly, and then they darken the air like a thick cloud; wherever any green appears, they drop down and settle on the spot. The noise they make in eating can be heard to a great distance, and the noise they make in flying is like the rustling of leaves in a forest. They cannot be destroyed: but there are two things they hate,—smoke and noise,—and by these they are sometimes scared and induced to fly away.

People and Customs.—Besides the wild animals, there are tame animals, who inhabit the steppe with men and women who take care of them. They are all wanderers, both men and beasts. You can easily guess why they wander. It is to find sufficient grass for the cattle.

Every six weeks the Tartars move to a new place. Yet one place is so like another, that no place appears new;—there is always the same immense plain—without a cottage, or an orchard, a green hill, or running brook, to make any spot remembered. It is great labor to the Tartar women to pack up the tents and to place them on the backs of the camels, and then to unpack and to pitch the tents. It is a great disgrace to the men to suffer the women to work as hard as they do: but the men are very idle, and like to sit by their tents smoking and drinking, while their wives are toiling and striving with all their might. The women have the care of all the cattle: and the men attend only to the horses. Perhaps they would not even do this, were it not that they are very fond of riding; and such riders as the Tartars are seldom seen.

To give you an idea how they ride, I will describe one scene that took place on the steppe.

Some travellers from Europe were on a visit to a Tartar prince: (for there are *princes* in the desert,) and they were taken to see a herd of wild horses. The prince wished to have one of these wild horses caught. It is not easy to do this. But Tartars know the way. Six men mounted a tame horse, and rushed into the midst of the wild horses. Each of the men had a great noose in his hand. They all looked at the prince to know which horse he would have caught. When they saw the prince give a sign, one of the men soon noosed a young horse. The creature seemed terrified when it found that it was caught: his eyes started out, his nostrils seemed to smoke. Presently a man came running up, sprang upon the back of the wild horse, and by cutting the straps round his neck, set him at liberty. In an instant the horse darted away with the swiftness of an arrow; yet the man firmly kept his seat. The animal seemed greatly alarmed at his strange burden, and tried every plan to get rid of it;—now suddenly stopping,—now crawling on the grass like a worm,—now rolling,—now rearing,—now dashing forward in a fast gallop through the midst of the herd; yet all would not do; the rider clung to the horse as closely as ever.

But how was the rider ever to get off his fiery steed? That would be difficult indeed; but help was sent to him by the prince. Two men on horseback rode after him, and between them they snatched away the man from the trembling and foaming horse. The animal, surprised to find his load suddenly gone, stood stupefied for a moment, and then darted off to join his companions. What *this* man did,—*many* Tartars can do: and even *little boys* will mount wild horses, and keep on by clinging to their manes: *women*, too, will gallop about on wild horses.

In Circassia the customs are very different; for though *men* ride so well, *women* there never ride at all; and surely it is far better not to ride than to be as bold as a Tartar woman.

FOOD.—What can be the food of the Tartars? Not bread, (for there is no corn,) nor fruit, nor vegetables. The flocks and herds are the food. The favorite meat is horse-flesh; though mutton and beef are eaten also. Then there is plenty of milk—both cow's milk and sheep's milk. As there is milk, there is butter and cheese. But it is very unwholesome to live on meat and milk without bread and vegetables. The water, too, is very bad; for it is taken from the muddy rivers, and not from clear springs. It is a comfort for the Tartar that he can procure tea from China. Their tea is indeed very unlike the tea brought to England; for it comes to Tartary in hard lumps, shaped like bricks. It is boiled in a saucepan with water, and then mixed with milk, butter, and salt. Thus you see the Tartar needs neither tea-kettle, teapot, nor sugar basin.

It would be well if tea and milk were the only drinks in Tartary; but a sort of spirit is distilled by the Tartars from mare's milk; and brandy also is brought from Russia.

Tents.—A Tartar tent is very unlike an Arab tent. It is in the shape of a hut, for the sides are upright, and the roof only is slanting, and there is a small hole at the top to let the smoke escape. Neither is it made of skins, but of thick woollen stuff, called felt, which keeps the cold out. At night the entrance is closed, and the family sleep on mats around the fire in the midst.

Appearance.—The Tartars are not handsome like the Turks and Circassians. They are short and thick; their faces are broad and bony, their eyes very small, and only half open; their noses flat, their lips thick, their chins pointed, their ears large and flapping, and their skin dark and yellow.

Their dress is warm, and well suited for riding in the desert. Different tribes have different dresses: this is the dress of the Kalmuck Tartar. He wears a yellow cloth cap trimmed with black lamb-skin; wide trowsers, a tight jacket, and over all a loose tunic, fastened round the waist. His boots are red, with high heels. The women dress like the men; but they let their hair grow in two long tresses, while the men shave part of their heads, and keep only *one* lock of hair hanging on their shoulders.

You see that the Tartars are much like the Chinese in their persons and dress; but they are a much stronger, bolder people, and much more ignorant. No wonder, therefore, that many years ago the Tartars got over the Chinese wall. and took possession of the Chinese throne. You must not forget that the Emperor of China is a Tartar.

GOVERNMENT.—To whom does Tartary belong? Has it a king of its own? No. Once it had many kings, called khans; but now the khans have lost their power, and are only *called* khan to do them honor. Now Tartary belongs to the great empires on each side of it,—Russia and China. Part of Tartary is called Russian Tartary, and part—Chinese Tartary. There is only a small part that is not conquered; and it is called Independent Tartary.

There are many different tribes, and each tribe keeps to a certain part of the land, and never ventures to wander beyond its own bounds.

RELIGION.—The religion is the same as that which is so common in China,—the religion of Buddha; but in some parts of Tartary there is the religion of Mahomet. It is sad to think that far more people in the world worship Buddha, the deceiver, than Jesus, the Son of God. The Tartars think to please their false god by making a loud noise. It would astonish a stranger to hear their jingling bells, shrill horns, squeaking shells, bellowing trumpets, and deafening drums. How unlike is their senseless noise to the sweet sound of a Christian hymn!

The Tartars think also to please their gods by glaring colors; so their priests dress in red and yellow, and bear flags, adorned with strips of gay silk. A band of priests looks something like a regiment of soldiers.

The chief priest is called the Lama, and he is worshipped as a god; but his situation is not very pleasant; for he is not allowed to walk without help. Whenever he attempts to walk, he is held up by a man on each side, as if he were an infant; and usually he is drawn in a car, or carried in a palanquin. From want of exercise, he becomes very weak and helpless. When he dies, his body is burned, and the ashes are gathered up and made into an idol. Thus he continues to be a god after he is dead. Another Lama is chosen by one of the princes. There are many Lamas in Tartary for the various tribes.

As the Tartars are always moving about, a tent serves for a temple; and the idols are carried in great chests. They cannot walk, therefore they must be carried. What use are such gods?

The Tartars have found out a way of praying without any trouble; and it is a way that suits idols very well. They get some prayers written, and place them in a drum, and then turn the drum round and round with a string. This they call praying; and while they are thus praying, they can be chattering, smoking, and even quarrelling. The princes have a still easier way of offering up prayers. They write prayers upon a flag, and then place it before their tents for the wind to blow it about.

This is *their* way of praying to their gods.

And what, my dear child, is *your* way of praying to your God?

Have missionaries visited the Tartars?

Yes; I will tell you of two German missionaries, who tried to convert a tribe of Tartars called the Kalmucks, living near the Caspian Sea and the river Volga. These good men were treated with great contempt by the Tartars. The missionaries translated the Gospel of St. Matthew into the Tartar language. One of the Tartars, instead of thanking them, observed, "I wonder you should take so much trouble to prepare a book that we shall never read." When the precious books were given to the Tartars, some of them returned the books; and when it was read to them, they scornfully said, as they turned away, "It is only the history of Jesus."

At last one Tartar, named Sodnom, believed in Jesus. He said to the missionaries, "Now the Tartars, from my example, may turn to the Lord: for as, when sheep are to be washed, each is afraid to enter the water till *one* has been in, so it may be with my countrymen."

Sodnom read every evening in the Testament to his family in the tent. At first his wife was displeased, and said that her husband wasted the fire-wood in making a light to read a book that was of no use. But afterwards she listened, and made the children keep quiet. The neighbors also listened, and *twenty-two* turned to the Lord!

Then the prince and the priests grew angry, and said the Christians must leave the camp. Where could the Christians go? There was a village called Sarepta, where some Germans lived. There they determined to go, though it was two hundred miles off. One of the missionaries led the way on horseback; the Tartars followed on foot: then came camels bearing the tents and the women, while a bullock-cart contained the young children. The flocks and herds were driven by the bigger children.

The good Germans in Sarepta received the Tartars with great joy. One gray-headed man of eighty-three came to meet them, leaning upon his staff. He said he had been praying that he might see a *Christian* Tartar before he died. He heard these Tartars sing hymns to the praise of Jesus, and he felt his prayers were answered. Two days afterwards he died. Like old Simeon, he might have said, "Lord, now lettest thou thy servant depart in peace, for mine eyes have seen thy salvation."

The Christians went to live in a small island in the river Volga. When the river was frozen, the Germans went over the ice to visit them. Sodnom gave them tea mixed with fat in a large wooden bowl; and to please him, the kind Germans drank some, though they did not like it. Many Tartars assembled in Sodnom's tent, and seated on the ground smoking their pipes, talked together about heavenly things; and before they parted, they put away their pipes, and folding their hands, sang hymns in their own language. The Germans, in taking leave, divided a large loaf among the company; for bread is considered quite a dainty by the Tartars.

The change that had taken place in these Tartars filled the Germans with joy; and more missionaries would have gone to teach the heathen Kalmucks, had not the Emperor of Russia forbidden them.

ASTRACAN.

This city is on the Caspian Sea. It is very unpleasant, on account of the heat and the gnats.

Not only Tartars dwell there, but many people of all nations, Russians, Hindoos, and Armenians. The chief trade of Astracan is in the fish of the sea, and in the salt on the shores.

BOKHARA (IN TARTARY).

This is a kingdom in the midst of Tartary. It lies at the south of the Caspian Sea. It is not like the rest of Tartary, for it is a sweet green spot. Travellers have said that it is the most beautiful spot in the world, but that is not true. The reason that travellers have said so, is that, after passing through a great desert, they have been charmed at seeing again running streams, and shady groves.

But though Bokhara is a beautiful place, it is a wicked place.

The king is one of the greatest tyrants in the world. He is called the Amir.

The city where he dwells is called Bokhara (which is also the name of the whole country). His palace is on a high mound, in the midst of splendid mosques, and mansions. Amongst these grand buildings is the prison, a place of horrible cruelty. There the prisoners lie in the dark, and the damp. One use of the prison is to keep water cool for the king in summer; it feels therefore just like a cellar.

But the worst dungeon, is filled with stinging insects, called "ticks," reared on purpose to torment prisoners. In order to keep the ticks alive when no prisoners are there, raw meat is thrown into the place. There is also a deep pit into which men are let down with ropes; as once the holy Jeremiah was in Jerusalem.

Once a fortnight the prisoners are judged by the Amir. Even when the ground is covered with snow they stand with bare feet, waiting for hours till the Amir appears.

Can so cruel a monarch be happy? No. He lives in constant fear of his life.

He is afraid of drinking water, lest it should be poisoned. All that he drinks is brought from the river in skins, and sealed, and guarded by two officers; it is then taken to the chief counsellor, called the Vizier, and tasted by him, and his servants; it is then sealed again, and sent to his majesty.

The Amir's dinner when it is ready, is not placed

on the royal table, but locked up in a box, and taken to the Vizier to be tasted, before it is served up in the palace.

But it is not the Amir only who is afraid of poison. No one will accept fruit from another, unless that other tastes it first. It must be very terrible to live in the midst of such murderers as the people of Bokhara seem to be.

The Amir is so much afraid of people making plans to destroy him, that he chooses to see all the letters that are written by his subjects; if a husband write to his wife, the letter must first be shown to the Amir. There are boys, too, going about the city listening to all that is said, that they may let the Amir know, if any one speak against him.

But while the Amir is watching his people, *they* are watching *him;* for his chief officers hire men to listen to the Amir's conversation, that they may know if he intends to kill them. Yet every person *appears* to approve all the Amir does, saying on every occasion, "It is the act of a king; it must be good." They are such people as Jeremiah describes in the Bible. "Their tongue is as an arrow shot out, it speaketh deceit; one *speaketh* peaceably to his neighbor, but in his *heart* he lieth his wait."—(Jer. ix. 8.)

APPEARANCE.—The people in Bokhara are much

handsomer than other Tartars; their complexions are fairer, and their hair is of a lighter color. They wear large white turbans, and several dark pelisses with high-heeled boots. These high heels prevent their walking well, and most people, both men and women, ride; but the ladies always hide their faces with a veil of black hair cloth.

The large court of the palace is filled from morning to night with a crowd of noisy people, most of them mounted on horses and donkeys.

In the midst of the court is the fruit market. It is wonderful to behold the quantity, and beauty of the fruits. The same fruits grow in Bokhara as in England, only they are much finer. *Such* grapes, plums, and apricots, mulberries, and melons, are never seen in Europe, and they are made more refreshing by being mixed with chopped ice. Large piles of ice stand all the summer long in the market-place, and even beggars drink iced water. But hot tea is preferred before any other drink. In every corner of the market there are large urns of hot tea, and small bowls of rich milk, surrounded all day by a thirsty crowd. How much better is this sight than the gin palaces of London!

But there is one great inconvenience in Bokhara, for which all its fruits can scarcely make amends.

There is bad water. For Bokhara is not built on the banks of a river, or among running brooks: all the water is brought by canals, from a small stream near the town, and when the canals are dried up by the heat, there is no water, except in the tanks where it is kept. This stagnant water produces a disease called the Guinea worm. In this complaint the skin is covered with painful swellings, and when they burst, a little flat worm is discovered in each, which must be drawn out before the poor sufferer can recover.

Religion.—It is the Mahomedan. The Amir is a strict observer of his religion. Every Friday he may be seen going to prayers in his great mosque. The Koran is carried before him, and four men with golden staves accompany him, crying out, "Pray to God that the Commander of the Faithful may act justly." As he passes by, his people stroke their beards to show their respect. Bokhara is reckoned by Mahomedans a very religious city; for in every street there is a mosque; every evening people may be seen crowding to prayers; and if boys are caught asleep during service, they are tied together, and driven round the market by an officer, who beats them all the way with a thick thong.

There is a school, too, in almost every street of Bokhara, and there the poor boys sit from sunrise, till an hour before sunset, bawling out their foolish lessons from the Koran; and during all that time they are never allowed to go home, except once for some bread. They have no time for play, except in the evening, and no holiday, except on Friday. Seven years they spend in this manner, learning to read and write. When they leave school, if they wish to be counted very wise, they go to one of the colleges; for there are many in Bokhara. Some spend all their lives in these colleges, living in small cells, and meeting in a large hall to hear lectures about the Mahomedan religion. It is a happy thing, however, that in summer the students go out to work in the fields; for how much better is it to work with the hands, than to fill the head with the wicked inventions of Mahomed.

The Mahomedans, however, are very proud of their religion, because they *say*, they do not worship idols; (yet they do worship at Mecca, a black stone, and other like things in other places). They imagine that *all* Christians are idolaters, for they know that the Russians bow down to pictures.

Once the Vizier of Bokhara conversed a long while with two Englishmen about their religion.

He asked them, "Do you worship idols?"

The Englishmen replied, "No."

The Vizier would not believe them, but said, "I

am sure you have images and crosses hung round your necks."

Upon which, they opened their vests to show there was nothing hidden.

Then the Vizier smiled, and said to his servants, "They are not bad people."

As the servants were preparing tea, the Vizier took a cup, and said to the travellers, "You must drink with us, for you are people of the Book," meaning the Bible.

Yet you must not suppose because the Vizier seemed to approve these Christians, that he, and the Amir, would allow missionaries to settle in the kingdom.

It is dangerous for Englishmen to visit Bokhara. When they do come, they must be very careful not to give offence, or they will lose their lives. Englishmen are more dreaded than any other people, because it is known in Bokhara, that they have conquered Hindostan, and therefore the Amir fears lest they should conquer his kingdom also. As soon as an Englishman enters Bokhara, he is forbidden to write a letter, for fear he should contrive some plan to bring enemies there. Neither is he allowed to ride in the streets; none but Mahomedans are allowed to ride in them, though any one may ride *outside* the city.

Some years ago two Englishmen came to Bokhara,

named Colonel Stoddart, and Captain Conolly. They acted foolishly in writing letters, and trying to send them secretly to their friends. They were found out, and shut up.

Colonel Stoddart behaved very wickedly in one respect; he pretended to be a Mahomedan! Was not this wicked? Soon he grew sorry, and declared himself a Christian. At last both Stoddart and Conolly were sentenced to die. They were led with their hands tied behind them to a place near the palace, to be executed. Conolly as he went along, cried out, "Woe, woe to me, for I have fallen into the hands of a tyrant." At the place of execution the two Englishmen kissed each other.

Stoddart said to the king's minister, (for the Amir was not present,) "Tell the Amir that I die a disbeliever in Mahomed, but a believer in Jesus. I am a Christian, and a Christian I die."

Then Conolly said to his friend, "We shall see each other in paradise near Jesus."

These were their last words. Immediately afterwards their heads were cut off with a knife.

Some time after this cruel murder, a clergyman, named Joseph Wolff, arrived at Bokhara. He had travelled all the way from England, and all alone, on purpose to inquire after Conolly, who had been his dear friend. The Amir was surprised at his coming, and said, "I have taken thousands of *Persians* and made them slaves, and no one came from Persia to inquire what was become of them; but as soon as I take two ENGLISHMEN prisoners, behold a man comes all this long way to inquire after *them!*"

The Amir did not know how precious are the lives of Englishmen in the eyes of their countrymen.

Joseph Wolff found it hard to get away from Bokhara. He was kept a long while in prison, and he feared he should be slain; for when he asked the Amir to give him the bones of Stoddart and Conolly to take to England, this was the Amir's answer: "I shall send YOUR bones!" Yet, after all, he was permitted to leave Bokhara, the Lord graciously inclining the tyrant to let him go.

How can Missionaries be sent to such a country!

Bokhara is the only large town in the kingdom.

The sea of Aral lies to the north of the kingdom: it is an immense lake, but not nearly so large as the Caspian Sea.

The river Oxus flows into the Caspian. It is famous for its golden sands.

The great trade of Bokhara is in black woolly lamb-skins, to make caps for the Persians: the younger the lamb the more delicate the wool. Thus many a pretty lambkin dies to adorn a Persian noble.

The best raisins in the world come from Bokhara.*

THE TOORKMAN TARTARS.

You have heard a great deal of the Tartars, and you have been told that they are a quiet and peaceable nation. But not *all;* there is a tribe of Tartars called the Toorkmans, of a very different character. They wander about in the country between Bokhara and Persia, and their chief employment is to steal men from Persia, and to sell them in Bokhara as slaves. A whole troop, mounted on horses, rush sword in hand upon a Persian city, and return to the camp with hundreds of beasts and human creatures as their captives.

Some English travellers once met five men chained together, walking with sad steps in the deep sands of the desert. They were Persians just caught by the Toorkmans, and on their way to Bokhara. When the Englishmen saw these poor captives, they uttered a sorrowful cry, and the Persians began to weep. One

* Taken from Sir Alexander Burnes, and from Kanikoff, the Russian, and from Rev. Joseph Wolff.

of the travellers stopped his camel to listen to their sad tale; and he heard that a few weeks before, while working in the fields, they had been seized and carried off. They were hungry and thirsty; for the Toorkmans cruelly starve their slaves, in order that they may be too weak to run away. The traveller gave them all he had, which was a melon, to quench their thirst.

But the worst part of the Toorkmans' conduct remains yet to be told. When they have taken many captives, they usually *kill* the old people, because they would not get much money for them in Bokhara; and they choose *one* of their captives to offer up as a thank-offering to their god!! Who is their god? The god of Mahomed. But though they are Mahomedans, they have no mosques, and are too ignorant to be able to read the Koran.

Robbery is their whole business. For this purpose they learn to ride and to fight. They understand well how to manage a horse, so as to make him strong and swift. They do not let him eat when he pleases, but they give him three meals a day of hay and barley, and then rein him up that he may not nibble the grass, and grow fat; and sometimes they give him no food at all, and yet make him gallop many miles. By this management the horses are very thin, but very *strong*, and able to bear their masters eighty miles in a day when required; and they are so swift that they can outrun their pursuers.

It is not surprising that the Toorkmans do not eat these thin horses, though other Tartars are so fond of horseflesh. They prefer mutton. When they invite a stranger to dinner, they boil a whole sheep in a large boiling-pot; then tear up the flesh,—mix it with crumbled bread, and serve it up in wooden bowls. Two persons eat from one bowl, dipping their hands into it, and licking up their food like dogs. The meal is finished by eating melons.

These coarse manners suit such fierce and wild creatures as the Toorkmans. It is their boast that they rest neither under the shadow of a TREE nor of a KING: meaning that they have neither trees nor kings to protect them in the desert.

The men wear high caps of black sheep-skin, while the women wear high white turbans. The tents are adorned with beautiful carpets, not only the floors, but the sides, and it is the chief employment of the women to weave them. As for the men, they spend most of their time in sauntering about among the tents; for the fierce dogs guard the flocks. But when their hands are idle, their thoughts are still busy in planning new robberies and murders.

It was by such men that the earth was inhabited when God sent the flood to destroy it. It is written, "The earth was filled with VIOLENCE."

Is there any man brave enough to go to these men to warn them of the judgment to come, and to tell them of pardon for the penitent, through the blood of Jesus?*

* Extracted from Sir Alexander Burnes' "Bokhara."

Chinese Tartary.

VERY little is known in Europe of this part of Tartary; and why? Because the Emperor of China, who reigns over it, does not like travellers to go there.

It is divided by high and snowy mountains from the rest of Tartary. When a traveller has passed over these mountains, he finds on the other side Chinese officers, who inquire what business he has come upon. If he have come only to wander about the country, he is desired to go home again; because the Chinese are afraid lest strangers should send spies, and then ARMIES—to conquer their empire.

One traveller, because he stayed too long in Tartary, was imprisoned for three months; and before he was let go, a picture of him was taken. What was done with this picture? It was copied, and the copies were sent to various towns on the borders of Chinese Tartary, with this command, "If the man, who is like this picture, enter the country, his head is the Emperor's, and his property is *yours.*" Happily the traveller heard of this command, and was never seen again in the country. You see how cunning it was of the Chinese to allow any one who killed the traveller to have his property; for thus they made it the interest of all to kill him.

There is one city in Chinese Tartary where many strangers come to trade with the people. It is called Yarkund. There caravans arrive from Pekin, laden with tea, after a journey of five months over the wilds of Tartary. Then merchants come from Bokhara to buy the tea, and to carrv it home, where it is so much liked.

Affghanistan.

This land is not a desert. Yet there are but few trees, and because there is so little shade, the rivulets are soon dried up. Yet it might be a fruitful land, if the inhabitants would plant and sow. But they prefer wandering about in tents, and living upon plunder, to settling in one place and living by their labor. The Tartar has good reason for roaming over his plains, because the land is bad; but the Affghan has no reason, but the *love* of roaming.

The plains of Affghanistan are sultry, but the mountains are cool; for their tops are covered with snow. The shepherds feed their flocks on the plains during the winter; but in the spring they lead them to the mountains to pass the summer there. Then the air is filled with the sweet scent of clover and violets. The sheep often stop to browse upon the fresh pasture; but they are not suffered to linger long. The children have the charge of the lambs; an old goat or sheep goes before to encourage the lambs to proceed, and the children follow with switches of green grass. Many a little child who can only just run alone, enjoys the sport of driving the young lambs. The tents are borne on the backs of camels. The men are terrible-looking creatures, tall, large, dark, and grim, with shaggy hair and long black beards. They wear great turbans of blue check and handsome jackets, and cloaks of sheep-skin; they carry in their girdles knives as large as a butcher's; and on their shoulders a shield and a gun.

Besides these wild wanderers, there are some Affghans who live in houses.

Cabool, the capital, is a fine city, and the king dwells in a fine citadel. The bazaar is the finest in all Asia. It is like a street with many arches across it; and these people sell all kinds of goods.

But what is a fine *bazaar* compared to a beautiful *garden?* Cabool is surrounded by gardens: the most beautiful is the king's. In the midst is an octagon summer-house, where eight walks meet, and all the walks are shaded by fruit-trees. Here grow, as in Bokhara, the best fruits to be found in an English garden, only much larger and sweeter. The same kind of birds, too, which sing in England sing among its branches, even the melodious nightingale. It is the chief delight of the people of Cabool to wander in the gardens: they come there every evening, after having spent the day in sauntering about the bazaar; for they are an idle people, talking much and working little.

The noise in the city is so great that it is difficult to make a friend hear what you say: it is not the noise of rumbling wheels as in London, for there are no wheeled carriages, but the noise of chattering tongues.

The Affghans are a temperate people; they live chiefly upon fruit with a little bread; and as they are Mahomedans, they avoid wine, and drink instead iced sherbets, made of the juice of fruits. In winter excellent *dried* fruits supply the place of fresh.

But the Affghan, though living on fruits, is far from being a harmless and amiable character; on the contrary, he is cruel, covetous, and treacherous. Much British blood has been shed in the valleys of Affghanistan.

We cannot blame the Affghans for defending their own country. It was natural for them to ask, "What right has Britain to interfere with us?"

A British army was once sent to Affghanistan to force the people to have a king they did not like, instead of one they did like.

I will tell you of a youth who accompanied his father to the wars. This boy looked forward with delight to going as a soldier to a foreign land, and his heart beat high when the trumpet sounded to summon the troops to embark. Joyfully he quitted Bombay, crossed the Indian Ocean, and landed near the mouth of the Indus. When the army began its march towards Affghanistan, he rode on a pony by his father's side.

At first it seemed pleasant to pitch the tent in a new spot every day, to rest during the heat, and to travel in the dead of the night, till the sun was high in the sky. But soon this way of life was found fatiguing, for the heat was great, and the water scarce. The air, too, was clouded by the dust the troops raised in marching; and green grass was seldom seen, or a shady tree under which to rest. The food, too, was dry and stale, and no fresh food could be procured, for the Affghans, before they fled, destroyed the corn and fruit growing in the fields, that their enemies might not eat them. The camels, too, which bore the baggage of the British army, grew ill from heat and thirst; for it is not true that camels can live *long* without water; in three or four days they die. Besides this, the hard rocks in the hilly country hurt their feet, and hastened their death. Many a camel died as it was seeking to quench its thirst at a narrow stream in the valley, and its dead body falling into the water, polluted it. Yet this water the soldiers drank, for they had no other, and from drinking it they fell ill. The father of the youthful soldier was one of these, and he was compelled to stop on the way for several weeks; and because the heat of a tent was too great, he took shelter in a ruined building. Here his son nursed him with a heavy heart. Where was the delight the youth had expected to find in a soldier's life?

At last the British army reached a strong fort built on the top of a hill; Guznee was its name. Its walls and gates were so strong that it seemed impossible to get into the city; yet the British knew that if they did *not*, they must die either by the Affghan sword, or by hunger and thirst among the rocks. For some time they were much perplexed and distressed. At last a thought came into the mind of a British captain, "Let us blow up the gates with gunpowder." The plan was good; but how to perform it,—there was the difficulty. Soon all was arranged. In the night some sacks of gunpowder were laid very softly against the gates; but as no one could set fire to the sacks when *close* to them, a long pipe of cloth was filled with gunpowder, and stretched like a serpent upon the ground; one end of the pipe touched the sack, and the other end was to be set on fire. But before the match was applied, a British officer peeped through a chink in the gates to see what the Affghans were doing within. Behold! they were quietly smoking, and eating their supper, not suspecting any danger! The match was applied—the gunpowder exploded, and the strong gates were shattered into a thousand pieces; the army rushed in sword in hand, and the Affghans fled in wild confusion.

Where was our young soldier? He was running into the fort between two friendly soldiers, who kindly helped him on; each of them was holding one of his arms, and assisting him to keep up with the troops, as they rushed through the gates. As he ran, he heard horrible cries, but the darkness hindered him from seeing the dying Affghans rolling in the dust, only he felt their soft bodies as he hastily passed over them. He heard his fellow-soldiers shouting and firing on every side. Some fell close beside him, and others were wounded, and carried off on the shoulders of their comrades, screaming with agony.

Half an hour after the gates were fired, the city was taken. The news of the victory spread among the Affghans on the mountains, and the plains, and the whole country submitted to the British.

The army soon marched to Cabool, that proud city. No one opposed their entrance, and the bazaar, and the king's garden, and the royal citadel were visited by our soldiers.

After spending two months in beautiful Cabool, resting their weary limbs and feasting on fine fruits, the army was ordered to return home. They began to march again towards the coast, a distance of fifteen hundred miles, over cragged rocks, and scorching plains.

In the course of this terrible journey, the father of the young soldier again fell ill, and was forced to stop by the way. His affectionate son nursed him night and day; closed his eyes in death, and saw him laid in a lowly grave in the desert. With a bleeding heart the youth embarked to return to Bombay.

During the voyage, a furious storm arose, and all on board despaired of life. *Then* it was the youth remembered the prayers he had offered up by his dying father's bed; *then* it was he felt he had not turned to God with all his heart, and *then* it was he vowed, that if the Lord would spare him this *once*, he would seek his face in truth. God heard and spared.

And did the youth remember his prayers and vows? He did, though not at *first*,—yet after a little while he *did*. He read the word of God, he prayed for the Spirit of God, and at length he enjoyed the peace of God; and now he neither fears storm nor sword, because Christ is his shelter and his shield.

Beloochistan.

JUST underneath Affghanistan, lies Beloochistan, by the sea coast. It is separated from India by the river Indus. You may know a Beloochee from an Affghan by his stiff red cotton cap, in the shape of a hat without a brim; whereas, an Affghan wears a turban. Yet the religion of the Beloochee is the same as that of the Affghan, namely, the Mahomedan, and the character is alike, only the Beloochee is the fiercer of the two: the country also is alike, being wild and rocky.

Beloochistan has not been conquered by the British: it has a king of its own; yet the British have fought against Beloochistan. On one occasion a British army was sent to punish the king of Beloochistan for not having sent corn to us, as he had promised.

The army consisted of three thousand men, and amongst them was the young soldier, of whom you have heard so much already. His father was ill at the time, and could not fight; but the youth came upon his pony, with a camel to carry his tent, and all his baggage.

The troops as usual marched in the night. In the morning, about eight o'clock, they first caught sight of Kelat, the capital of Beloochistan. It was a grand sight, for the city is built on a high hill, with a citadel at the top. The dark Beloochees were seen thronging about the walls and the towers, gazing at the British army, but not daring to approach them.

Our soldiers, when they first arrived, were too much tired to begin the attack, and therefore they rested on the grass for two hours. At ten o'clock the word of command was given, and the attack was made. The British planted their six cannons opposite the gates, and began to fire.

Where was the young soldier? He was commanded to run with his company close up to the wall, and there to remain. As he ran, he was exposed to the full fire of the enemy. The youth heard bullets whizzing by as he passed, and he expected every moment that some ball would lay him low; but through the mercy of God he reached the wall in safety. *Close* underneath the wall was not a dangerous post, for the bullets passed over the heads of those standing there.

About noon, the British cannons had destroyed the gates. Then the British soldiers rushed into the town. Amongst the first to enter was the young soldier; because when the gates fell he was standing close by. As he passed along the streets, he saw no one but the dead and the dying for the Beloochees had fled for refuge to their citadel on the top of the hill. The king himself was there.

The citadel was a place very difficult for an enemy to enter; for the entrance was through a narrow dark passage underground. Into this passage the British soldiers poured, but soon they came to a door, which they could not get through, for Beloochee soldiers stood there, sword in hand, ready to cut down any one who approached. "Look at my back," said one soldier to his fellow. The other looked, and beheld the most frightful gashes gaping wide and bleeding freely. Such were the wounds that each soldier, who ventured near that door, was sure to receive.

At this momeat a cry was heard, saying, "Another passage is found." When the Beloochees heard this cry, they gave up all hopes of keeping the enemy out of the citadel; so they left off fighting, and cried "Peace."

But their king was already dead; he had fallen on the threshold of the passage last found. The *first* man who tried to get in by that way the *king* had killed; but the *second* had killed the king. The British, as they rushed in by this new way, trampled on the body of the fallen monarch. He was a splendid object even in death; his long dark ringlets were flowing over his glittering garments, and his sharp sword, with its golden hilt, was in his hand. The British hurried by, and climbed the steep and narrow stairs leading to the top of the citadel, and the enemy no longer durst oppose their course.

On the terrace at the top of the citadel, in the open air, stood the nobles of Beloochistan. There were princes too from the countries all around. It was a magnificent assembly. These men were the finest of a fine race. Some were clad in shining armor, and others in flowing garments of green and gold. Thus they stood for *a moment*, and the *next*—they were rolling on the ground!!

How was this? Had not peace been agreed upon on both sides? Yes, but a British soldier had attempted to take away the sword of one of the princes. The prince had resisted, and with his sword, had wounded the soldier; and instantly every British gun on that spot had been pointed at the nobles of Beloochistan.

This was why the nobles were lying in the agonies of death.

Our young soldier was not one of those who slew the nobles. He was standing on another part of the terrace, when, hearing a tremendous volley of guns, he exclaimed to a friend, "What can that be?" Going forward, he beheld heaps of bleeding bodies, turbans, and garments—in one confused mass. The dying were calling for water, and the very soldiers who had shot them, were holding cups to their quivering lips, though themselves parched with thirst. But water could not save the lives of the fallen nobles: one by one they ceased to cry out, and soon—all were silent —and all were still. The VICTORY was WON! But how awful had been the last scene! How cruelly, how unjustly, had the lives of that princely assembly been cut short!

The conquerors returned that evening to their camp. On their way, they passed through the desolate streets of the city; the mud cottages on each side were empty, and blood flowed between. The young officer, as he marched at the head of his company, was struck by seeing a row of his own fellow-soldiers lying dead upon the ground. They had been placed there ready for burial on the morrow. Their ghastly faces, and gaping wounds were terrible to behold. The youth remembered them full of life and spirits in the morning, unmindful of their dismal end; *then* he felt how merciful God had been in sparing his life; and when he crept into his little tent that night, he returned him thanks upon his knees; though he did not love him *then* as his Saviour from eternal death. Wearied, he soon fell asleep, but his sleep was broken by dreadful dreams of blood and death.

The next day he walked through the conquered town, and saw the British soldiers dragging the dead bodies of their enemies by ropes fastened to their feet. They were dragging them to their grave, which was a deep trench, and there they cast them in and covered them up with earth.

Such is the history of the conquest of Kelat.* How many souls were suddenly hurled into eternity! How many unprepared to meet their Judge, because their sins were unpardoned, and their souls unwashed! But in war, who thinks of souls and sins! O horrible war How hateful to the Prince of Peace!

* September 13, 1839.

Burmah.

Of all the kings in Asia, the king of Burmah is the greatest, next to the emperor of China. He has not indeed nearly as large a kingdom, or as many subjects as that emperor; but like him, he is worshipped by his people. He is called "Lord of life and death," and the "Owner of the sword," for instead of holding a *sceptre* in his hand, he holds a golden sheathed *sword*. A sword indeed suits him well, for he is very cruel to his subjects. Nowhere are such severe punishments inflicted. For drinking brandy the punishment is, pouring molten lead down the throat; and for running away from the army, the punishment is, cutting off both legs, and leaving the poor creature to bleed to death. A man for choosing to be a Christian was beaten all over the body with a wooden mallet, till he was one mass of bruises; but before he was dead, he was let go.

Every one is much afraid of offending this cruel king. The people tremble at the sound of his name;

and when they see him, they fall down with their heads in the dust. The king makes any one a lord whom he pleases, yet he treats even his lords very rudely. When displeased with them, he will hunt them out of the room with his drawn sword. Once he made forty of his lords lie upon their faces for several hours, beneath the broiling sun, with a great beam over them to keep them still. It was well for them that the king did not send for the men with spotted faces. Who are those men? The executioners. Their faces are always covered with round marks tattooed in the skin. The sight of these spotted faces fills all the people with terror. Every one runs away at the sight of a spotted face, and no one will allow a man with a spotted face to sit down in his house. In what terror the poor Burmese must live, not knowing when the order for death will arrive. Yet the king is so much revered, that when he dies, instead of saying, "He is dead," the people say, "He is gone to amuse himself in the heavenly regions."

The king has a great many governors under him, and they are as cruel as himself. A missionary once saw a poor creature hanging on a cross. He inquired what the man had done, and finding that he was not a murderer, he went to the governor to entreat him to pardon the man. For a long while the governor refused to hear him: but at last he gave him a note, desiring the crucified man to be taken down from the cross. Would you believe it?—the Burmese officers were so cruel that they would not take out the nails, till the missionary had promised them a *piece of cloth* as a reward! When the man was released, he was nearly dead, having been seven hours bleeding on the cross; but he was tenderly nursed by the missionary, and at last he recovered. Yet all the agonies of a cross had not changed the man's heart, and he returned to his old way of life as a thief. Had he believed in that Saviour who was nailed to a cross for his sins, he would, like the dying thief, have repented.

Though the Burmese are so unfeeling to each other, they think it wrong to kill animals, and never eat any meat, except the flesh of animals who have died of themselves. Even the fishermen think they shall be punished hereafter for catching fish; but they say, "We must do it, or we shall be starved." You may be sure that such a people must have some false and foolish religion; and so they have, as you will see.

Religion.—It is the religion of Buddha. This Buddha was a man who was born at Benares, in India, more than two thousand years ago; and people say, that for his great goodness was made a boodh, or a god. Yet the Burmese do not think he is alive

IDOL CAR AND PAGODA.

p. 203

now; they say he is resting as a reward for his goodness. Why then do they pray to him, if he cannot hear them? They pray because they think it is very good to pray, and that they shall be rewarded for it some day. What reward do they expect? It is this —to *rest* as Buddha does—to sleep forever and ever. This is the reward they look for. Every one in Burmah thinks he has been born a great many times into the world,—now as an insect,—now as a bird,—now as a beast, and he thinks that because he was very good,—as a reward he was made a *man*. Then he thinks that if he is very good as a *poor* man, he shall be born next time to be a *rich* man; and at last, that he will be allowed to rest like Buddha himself. What is it to be good? The Burmese say that the greatest goodness is making an idol, and next to that, making a pagoda. You know what an idol is, but do you know what a pagoda is? It is a house, with an idol *hidden* inside, and it has no door, nor window, therefore no one can get into a pagoda. Some pagodas are very large, and others very small. As it is thought so very good to make idols and pagodas, the whole land is filled with them; the roads in some places are lined with them; the mountains are crowned with them.

Next to making idols, and building pagodas, it is considered good to make offerings. You may see the father climbing a steep hill to reach a pagoda, his little one by his side, and plucking green twigs as he goes. He reaches the pagoda, and strikes the great bell, then enters the idol-house near the pagoda, and teaches his young child how to fold its little hands, and to raise them to its forehead, while it repeats a senseless prayer; then leaving the green twigs at the idol's feet, the father descends with his child in his arms. How many little ones, such as Jesus once took in his arms, are taught every day to serve Satan.

The people who are thought the best in Burmah, are the priests. Any one that pleases may be a priest. The priests pretend to be poor, and go out begging every morning with their empty dishes in their hands; but they get them well filled, and then return to the handsome house, all shining with gold, in which they live together in plenty and in pride. They are expected to dress in rags, to show that they are poor; but not liking rags, they cut up cloth in little pieces, and sew the pieces together to make their yellow robes; and this they call wearing rags. They pretend to be so modest, that they do not like to show their faces, and so hide them with a fan, even when they preach; for they do preach in their way, that is, they tell foolish stories about Buddha. The name they give him is Guadama, while the Chinese call him Fo. They have five hundred and fifty stories written in their books about him; for they say he was once a bird, a fly, an elephant, and all manner of creatures, and was so good whatever he was, that at last he was born the son of a king.

CHARACTER.—The Burmese are a blunt and rough people. They are not like the Chinese and the Hindoos, ready to pay compliments to strangers. When a Burmese has finished a visit, he says, "I am going," and his friend replies, "Go." This is very blunt behavior. But all blunt people are not sincere. The Burmese are very deceitful, and tell lies on every occasion; indeed, they are not ashamed of their falsehoods. They are also very proud, because they fancy they were so good before they were born into this world. All the kind actions they do are in the hope of getting more merit, and this bad motive spoils all they do. They are kind to travellers. In every village there is a pretty house, called a Zayat, where travellers may rest. As soon as a guest arrives, the villagers hasten to wait upon him;—one brings a clean mat, another a jug of water, and a third a basket of fruit. But why is all this attention shown? In the hope of getting merit. The Burmese resemble the Chinese in their respect to their parents. They are better than the Chinese in their treatment of their children, for they are kind to the *girls* as well as to the boys; neither do they destroy any of their infants. They are temperate also, not drinking wine,—having only two meals in the day, and then not eating too much. In these points they are to be approved. They are, however, very violent in their tempers; it is true they are not very easily provoked, but when they are angry, they use very abusive language. Thus you see they are by no means an amiable people.

APPEARANCE.—In their persons they are far less pleasing than the Hindoos; for instead of *slender* faces and figures, they have broad faces and thick figures. But they have not such dark complexions as the Hindoos.

They disfigure themselves in various ways. To make their skins yellow, they sprinkle over them a yellow powder. They also make their teeth black, because they say they do not wish to have white teeth like dogs and monkeys. They bore their ears, and put bars of gold, or silver, or marble through the holes.

The women wear a petticoat and a jacket. The men wear a turban, a loose robe, and a jacket; they tie up their hair in a knot behind, and tattoo their legs, by pricking their skin, and then putting in black oil. They have the disagreeable custom of smoking, and of chewing a stuff called "coon," which they carry in a box.

Every one (except the priests) carries an umbrella to guard him from the sun; the king alone has a white one; his nobles have gilded umbrellas; the next class have red umbrellas; and the lowest have green.

Food.—Burmah is a pleasanter country than Hindostan, for it is not so hot, and yet it is as fruitful. The people live chiefly upon rice; but when they cannot get enough, they find abundance of leaves and roots to satisfy their hunger.

Animals.—There are many tigers, but no lions. The Burmese are fond of adorning their houses with statues of lions, but never having seen any, they make very strange and laughable figures. The pride of Burmah is her elephants; but they all belong to the king, and none may ride upon one but himself, and his chief favorite. Carriages are drawn by bullocks, or buffaloes; and there are horses for riding, so the Burmese can do very well without the elephants. The king thinks a great deal too much of these noble animals. There was a white elephant that he delighted in so much, that he adorned it with gold, and jewels, and counted it next to himself in rank, even above the queen.

Houses.—The Burmese build their houses on posts, so that there is an empty place under the floors. Dogs and crows may often be seen walking under the houses, eating whatever has fallen through the cracks of the floor.

The king allows none but the nobles to build houses of brick and stone; the rest build them of bamboos. This law is unpleasant; but there is another law which is a great comfort to the poor. It is *this*;— any one may have land who wishes for it. A man has only to cultivate a piece of spare land, and it is counted his, *as long* as he continues to cultivate it; therefore all industrious people have gardens of their own.

THE KARENS.

Among the mountains of Burmah, there are a wild people called the Karens, very poor and very ignorant; yet some have attended to the voice of the missionaries. They are not so proud as the Burmese; for they have no gods at all, and no books at all: they have not filled their heads with five hundred and fifty stories about Gaudama; therefore they are more ready to listen to the history of Jesus.

The Karens live in houses raised from the ground,

and so large is the place underneath, that they keep poultry and pigs there. Every year they move to a new place, and build new houses, clear a new piece of ground, by burning the weeds, dig it up, and sow rice. Thus they wander about, and they number their years by the number of houses they have lived in.

Of all the Eastern nations, they sing and play the most sweetly, and when they become Christians, they sing hymns, very sweetly indeed.

There is one Christian village among the mountains, called Mata, which means love; and every morning the people meet together in the Zayat, or travellers' house, to sing and pray. Before they were Christians, the Karens were in constant fear of the Nats; (not *insects*, but evil spirits), and sometimes in order to please their Nats, they were so cruel as to beat a pig to death. The Christian Karens have left off such barbarous practices, and have become kind and compassionate. When the missionaries told them that they ought to love one another, some of them went secretly the next day to wait upon a poor leper, and upon a woman covered with sores. Another day, without being asked, they collected some money and brought it to the missionaries, saying, they wished to set free a poor Burman who had been imprisoned for

Christ's sake. It is cheering to the missionaries to see them turning from their sins.*

AVA.

This city was once the capital of Burmah, and then it was called the "golden city." But now the king lives in another city, and the glory of Ava has passed away.

MAULMAIN.

This city, though in Burmah, may be called a British city, because the British built it; for they have conquered great part of Burmah. There are missionaries there. One there is, named Judson, who has turned more than a hundred Burmese to the Lord. But he has known great troubles. His wife and his little girl shared in these troubles.

I will now relate the history of the short life of little Maria Judson.

* Taken from "Travels in Eastern Asia," by Rev. Howard Malcolm.

THE MISSIONARY'S BABE.

The missionary's babe, little Maria, was born in a cottage by the side of a river, and very near the walls of the great city of Ava, where the king dwelt.

It was a wooden cottage, thatched with straw, and screened by a verandah from the burning sun. It was not like an English cottage, for it was built on high posts, that the cool air might play beneath. It contained three small rooms all on one floor. The country around was lovely; for the green banks of the river were adorned with various colored flowers and with trees laden with fine fruits.

In this pretty cottage, the infant Maria was lulled in her mother's arms to sleep, and often the tears rolling down the mother's cheeks, fell upon the baby's fair face. Why did the mother weep? It was for her husband she wept. He was not dead, but he was in prison. He was a missionary, and the king of Ava had imprisoned him in the midst of the great city. Was his wife left all alone with her babe in her cottage? No, there were two little Burmese girls there. They were the children of heathen parents, and they had been received by the kind lady into her cottage, and now they were learning to worship God. Their new names were, Mary, and Abby. There were also two men servants, of dark complexion, dressed in white cotton, and wearing turbans. It was a sorrowful little household, because the master of the family was absent, because he was in distress, and his life was in danger. Every day his fond wife visited him in his prison. She left her babe under the care of Mary, and set out with a little basket in her hand. After walking two miles through the streets of Ava, she came to some high walls—she knocked at the gate—a stern-looking man opened it. The lady, passing through the gates, entered a court. In one corner of the court, there was a little shed made of bamboos, and near it, upon a mat, sat a pale, and sorrowful man. His countenance brightens when he perceives the lady enter. She refreshes him with the nice food she has brought in her basket, and comforts him with sweet and heavenly words:—then hastens to return to her babe. As soon as she enters her cottage, she sinks back, half fainting, in her rocking-chair, while she folds again her little darling in her arms. Happy babe! thy parents are suffering for Jesus—and they are blessed of the Lord, and their baby with them.

Greater sorrows still, soon befell the little family. One day, a messenger came to the cottage, with the sad tidings that the bamboo hut had been torn down, the mat, and pillow taken away, and the prisoner, laden with chains, thrust into the inner prison. The loving wife hastened to the governor of the city to ask for mercy; but she could obtain none, only she was permitted to see her husband. And *what* a sight! He was shut up in a room with a hundred men, and without a *window*!! Though the weather was hot no breath of air reached the poor prisoners, but through the cracks in the boards. No wonder that the missionary soon fell ill of a fever. His wife, fearing he would die, determined to act like the widow in the parable, and to weary the unjust judge by her entreaties. She left her quiet cottage, and built a hut of bamboos at the governor's gate, and there she lived with her babe, and the little Burmese girls. The prison was just opposite the governor's gate, so that the anxious wife had now the comfort of being near her suffering husband. The governor was wearied by her importunity, and at last permitted her to build again a bamboo hovel for the prisoner in the court of the prison. The sick man was brought out of the noisome dungeon, and was laid upon his mat in the fresh air. He was supplied with food and medicine by his faithful wife, and he began to recover.

But in three days, a change occurred. Suddenly the poor wife heard that her beloved had been dragged from his prison, and taken, she knew not where. She inquired of everybody she saw, "Where is he gone?" but no answer could she obtain. At last the governor told her, that his prisoner was taken to a great city, named A-ma-ra-poora. This city was seven miles from Ava. The wife decided in a moment what to do. She determined to follow her husband. Taking her babe in her arms, and accompanied by the Burmese children, and one servant, she set out. She went to the city up the river in a covered boat, and thus she was sheltered from the scorching sun of an Indian May. But when she arrived at Amarapoora, she heard that her husband had been taken to a village six miles off. To this village she travelled in a clumsy cart drawn by oxen. Overcome with fatigue, she arrived at the prison, and saw her poor husband sitting in the court chained to another prisoner, and looking very ill. He had neither hat, nor coat, nor shoes, and his feet were covered with wounds he had received, as he had been driven over the burning gravel on the way to the prison: but his wounds had been bound up by a kind heathen servant, who had torn up his own turban to make bandages.

When the missionary saw his wife approaching with her infant, he felt grieved on her account, and exclaimed, "Why have you come? You cannot live here?" But she cared not where she lived, so that she could be near her suffering husband. She wished to build a bamboo hut at the prison gate: but the jailor would not allow her. However, he let her live in a room of his own house. It was a wretched room, with no furniture but a mat. Here the mother and the children slept that night, while the servant, wrapped in his cloth, lay at the door. They had no supper that night. Next day, they bought food in the village, with some silver that the lady kept carefully concealed in her clothes.

A new trouble soon came upon them. Mary was seized with a small-pox of a dreadful sort. Who now was to help the weak mother to nurse the little Maria? Abby was too young. The babe was four months old, and a heavy burden for feeble arms; yet all day long the mother carried it, as she went to and fro from the sick child to the poor prisoner. Sometimes, when it was asleep, she laid it down by the side of her husband. He was able to watch a *sleeping* babe, but not to nurse a babe *awake*, owing to his great weakness, and to his mangled feet. Soon the babe herself was attacked by the small-pox, and continued very ill for three months. This last trial was too much for the poor mother. Her strength failed her, and for many weeks she lay upon her mat unable to rise. She must have perished, if it had not been for the faithful servant. He was a native of Bengal, and a heathen. Yet he was so much concerned for his sick mistress and imprisoned master, that he would sometimes go without food all day, while he was attending to their wants; and he did all without expecting any wages.

The poor little infant was in a sad case, now its mother was lying on the mat. It cried so much for milk, that once its father got leave to carry it round the village to ask the mothers who had babes, to give some milk to his. By this plan, the little creature was quieted in the day, but at night its cries were most distressing.

The time at length arrived, when these trials were to end. The king sent for the missionary, not to put him to death, as he had once intended, but to ask for his help. What help could he render to the king! The reason why the missionary had been imprisoned so long was, that a British army had attacked Burmah. The king had feared, lest the missionary should take part with the enemy, and therefore he had shut him up. Now there were hopes of peace, and an interpreter was wanted to help the Burmese to speak with the British. The missionary knew both the English language and the Burmese, and he could explain to the king what the English general would say.

For this purpose he was brought to Ava. He was not driven along the road like a beast, but relieved from his chains, and treated with less cruelty than formerly. Yet he was still a prisoner.

The mother was now well enough to make a journey, though still very weak. She returned to her cottage by the river-side, and soon she had the delight of seeing her husband enter it. It was seventeen months since he had been torn from it by the king's officers, and ever since, he had been groaning in irons. But he was not now come to remain in his cottage, but only to obtain a little food and clothing to take with him to the Burmese camp. His wife felt cheered on his account, hoping that as an interpreter he would be well treated.

No sooner was he gone, than she was seized with that deadly disease, called spotted fever. What now would become of little Maria? Through the tender mercy of God, on the very day the mother fell ill, a Burmese woman offered to nurse the babe. Every day the mother grew worse, till at last the neighbors came in to see her die. As they stood around, they exclaimed, in their Burmese tongue, "She is dead, and if the king of angels should come in, he could not recover her." *Their* king of angels could *not*, but *her* KING of ANGELS could, for he can raise the dead.

But this dear lady was *not* dead, though nearly dead.

The Lord of life showed her mercy. A friend entered the sick chamber. It was Dr. Price, a missionary and a prisoner, but who had obtained leave from the king to visit the sick lady. He understood her case, and he ordered her head to be shaved, and blisters to be applied to her feet. From that time, she began to recover, and in a month, she had strength to stand up. The governor, who had once been so slow to hear her complaints, now sent for her to his house. He reeeived her in the kindest manner. What was her joy, when she found her husband there, not as a prisoner, but as a guest. Many prayers had she offered up, during her long illness, and they were now answered. The promise she had trusted in was fulfilled. This was *that* promise: "Call upon me in the day of trouble, and I WILL DELIVER THEE, and thou shalt glorify me."

But still brighter days were at hand. The King of Burmah had peace with the British, and had agreed to deliver the missionaries into their hands. Glad, indeed, were they to escape from the power of the cruel monarch. Little Maria and her parents, as well as Mary and Abby, were conveyed in a boat down the river to the place where the English army had encamped. The English general received them with fatherly kindness, and gave them a tent to dwell in near his own. What a fortnight they spent in that tent. It was a morning of joy, after a night of weeping. Little Maria was now, for the first time, dwelling with *both* her parents.

Soon afterwards she was taken to a new home in a town in Burmah, built by the English. It was called Amherst.* Here the missionary might teach the Burmese to know their Saviour, without being under the power of the cruel Burmese king.

It seemed as if the little family, so long afflicted, were now to dwell in safety, and to labor in comfort. But there is a rest for the people of God, and to this rest one of this family was soon removed.

The missionary determined to go to Ava, to plead with the king for permission to teach his subjects. He parted from his beloved wife, little thinking he should never see her again.

During her husband's absence, she watched with deep anxiety over her little Maria. The child was pale, and puny, yet very affectionate and intelligent. Whenever her mamma said, "Where is dear papa gone?" the little creature started up, and pointed to

* Amherst is only thirty miles from Maulmain.

the sea. She could not speak plainly, for she was only twenty months old.

Not long did she enjoy her mother's tender care. The poor mother, worn with her past watching, and weeping, was attacked by fever. As she lay upon the bed, she was heard to say, "The teacher is long in coming, I must die alone, and leave my little one; but as it is the will of God, I am content."

She grew so ill, that she took no notice of anything that passed around her; but even then she called for her child, and charged the nurse to be kind to it, and to indulge it in everything till its father returned. This charge she gave, because she knew the babe was sick, and needed the tenderest care. At last the mother lay without moving, her eyes closed, and her head resting on her arm. Thus she continued for two days, and then she uttered one cry, and ceased to breathe. Her illness had lasted eighteen days. Then she rested from her labors, and slept in Jesus.

What now became of little Maria? The wife of an English officer received her in her house for a few weeks, and then a missionary and his wife came to Maria's home, and took charge of the child. Maria was pleased to come back to her own home, and she fancied that kind Mrs. Wade was her own mother.

What a day it was when the poor father returned

home! No wife to meet him, with love and joy; only a sickly babe, who had forgotten him, and turned from him with alarm. Where could he go, but to the grave to weep there? then he returned to the house to look at the very spot where he had knelt with his wife in prayer, and parted from her in hope of a happy return.

Little Maria was nursed with a mother's care, though not in a mother's arms; but her delicate frame had been shaken by her infant troubles, and care and comforts came TOO LATE. After drooping day by day, she died at the age of two years and three months, exactly six months after her mother. Her father was near to close her faded eyes, and fold her little hands on her cold breast, and then to lay her in a little grave, close beside her mother's, under the Hope Tree.

The words of the poet would suit well the case of this much tried infant:—

> "Short pain, short grief, dear babe, were thine,
> *Now*, joys eternal and divine."

Like Maria's are the sufferings of many a missionary's babe, and many lie in an early tomb. But they are dear to the Saviour, for their parents' sakes, and their deaths are precious in his sight, and their spirits and their dust are safe in his hands.

Siam.

CROSS a river, and you pass from Burmah to Siam. These two countries, like most countries close together, have quarrelled a great deal, and now Britain has got in between them, and has parted them; as a nurse might come and part two quarrelsome children. Britain has conquered that part of Burmah which lies close to Siam, and has called it British Burmah; so Siam is now at peace.

But though these two countries have been such enemies, they are as like each other as two sisters. Siam is the little sister. Siam is a long narrow slip of a country, having the sea on one side, and mountains on the other.

The religion of Siam is the same as that of Burmah, the worship of Buddha. But in Siam he is not called Buddha: the name given him there is "Codom." You see how many names this Buddha has; in China he is Fo; in Burmah he is Gaudama; in Siam, he is Codom. Neither is he honored in Siam in exactly the same way as in Burmah. Instead of building magnificent pagodas, the Siamese build magnificent image houses or temples.

The Siamese resemble the Burmese in appearance, but they are much worse looking. Their faces are very broad, and flat; and so large are the jaws under the ears, that they appear as if they were swollen. Their manner of dressing their hair does not improve their looks; for they cut their hair quite close, except just on the top of their heads, where they make it stand up like bristles; nor do they wear any covering on their heads, except when it is very hot, and then they put on a hat, in the shape of a milk pan, made of leaves. They do not disfigure themselves, as the Burmese do, with nose-rings, and ear-bars; but they love ornaments quite as much, and load themselves with necklaces and bracelets. Their dress consists of a printed cotton garment, wound round the body. This is the dress of the women as well as of the men; only sometimes the women wear a handkerchief over their necks.

In disposition the Siamese are deceitful, and cowardly. It has been said of them, that as *friends* they are not to be *trusted*, and as *enemies* not to be *feared*: they cannot be trusted because they are deceitful: they need not be feared because they are cowardly

This is indeed a dreadful character; for many wicked people are faithful to their friends, and brave in resisting their enemies.

No doubt the manner in which they are governed makes them cowardly; for they are taught to behave as if they were worms. Whoever enters the presence of the king, must creep about on hands and knees. The great lords require their servants to show them the same respect. Servants always crawl into a room, pushing in their trays before them; and when waiting, they walk about on their knees. How shocking to see men made like worms to gratify the pride of their fellow-men! The rule is never to let your head be higher than the head of a person more honorable than yourself; if he stand, you must sit; if he sit, you must crouch.

The Siamese are like the Burmese in cruelty. When an enemy falls into their hands, no mercy is shown.

A king of a small country called Laos, was taken captive by the Siamese. This king, with his family, were shut up in a large iron cage, and exhibited as a sight. There he was, surrounded by his sons and grandsons, and all of them were heavily laden with chains on their necks and legs. Two of them were little boys, and they played and laughed in their cage!—so thoughtless are children! But the elder sons looked very miserable; they hung down their heads, and fixed their eyes on the ground; and well they might; for within their sight were various horrible instruments of torture;—spears with which to pierce them;—an iron boiler, in which to heat oil to scald them;—a gallows on which to hang their bodies, and—a pestle and mortar in which to pound the children to powder. You see how Satan fills the heart of the heathen with his own cruel devices. The people who came to see this miserable family, rejoiced at the sight of their misery: but they lost the delight they expected in tormenting the old king, for he died of a broken heart; and all they could do *then*, was to insult his body; they beheaded it, and then hung it upon a gibbet, where every one might see it, and the beasts and birds devour it.

What became of his unhappy family is not known.

But though so barbarous to their *enemies*, the Siamese in some respects are better than most other heathen nations, for they treat their *relations* more kindly. They do not kill their infants, nor shut up their wives, nor cast out their parents. Yet they show their cruelty in this:—they often sell one another for slaves. They also purchase slaves in great numbers; and there are wild men in the mountains who watch Burmans and Karens to sell them to the great chiefs of Siam. It is the pride of their chiefs to have thousands of slaves crawling around them.

BANKOK.

This city is built on an island in a broad river, and part of it on the banks of the river. It ought therefore to be a pleasant city, but it is *not*, owing to its extreme untidiness. The streets are full of mud, and overgrown with bushes, amongst which all the refuse is thrown; there are also many ditches with planks thrown across. There is only one pleasant part of the town, and that is, where the Wats are built. The Wats are the idol-houses. Near them are shady walks and fragrant flowers, and elegant dwellings for the priests. The people think they get great merit by making Wats, and therefore they take so much trouble: for the Siamese are very idle. So idle are they that there would be very little trade in Bankok, if it were not for the Chinese, who come over here in crowds, and make sugar, and buy and sell, and get money to take back to China. You may tell in a moment a Chinaman's garden from a Siamese garden;

one is so neat and full of flowers;—the other is overgrown with weeds and strewn with litter.

The most curious sight in Bankok, is the row of floating houses. These houses are placed upon posts in the river, and do not move about as boats do; yet if you *wish* to move your house, you can do so; you have only to take up the posts, and float to another place.

Besides the floating houses, there are numerous boats in the river, and some so small that a child can row them. There are so many that they often come against each other, and are overset. A traveller once passed by a boat where a little girl of seven was rowing, and by accident his boat overset hers. The child fell out of her boat, and her paddle out of her hand; yet she was not the least frightened, only surprised; and after looking about for a moment, she burst out a laughing, and was soon seen swimming behind her boat (still upside down), with her paddle in her hand. These little laughing rowers are too giddy to like learning, and they are not at all willing to come to the missionaries' schools; but some poor children, redeemed from slavery, are glad to be there, and have been taught about Christ in these schools.

Malacca.

This is a peninsula, or almost an island, for there is water almost all round it. In shape it is something like a *dog's* leg, even as Italy is like a *man's* leg.

The weather in Malacca is much pleasanter than in most parts of India, because the sea-breezes make the air fresh. There is no rainy season, as in most hot countries, but a shower cools the air almost every day. The country, too, is beautiful, for there are mountains, and forests, and streams.

Yet it is a dangerous country to live in, for the people are very treacherous. There are many pirates among them. What are pirates? Robbers by sea. If they see a small vessel, in a moment the pirates in their ships try to overtake it, seize it, take the crew prisoners, and sell them for slaves. The governors of the land do not punish the pirates; far from punishing them, they share in the gains. That is a wicked land indeed, where the governors encourage the people in their sins.

Malacca has no king of her own; the land belongs to Siam, except a very small part. The inhabitants are called Malays. They are not like the Siamese in character; for instead of being cowardly, they are fierce. Neither have they the same religion, for instead of being Buddhists, they are Mahomedans. Yet they know very little about the Koran, or its laws. One command, however, they have learned, which is—to hate infidels. They count all who do not believe in Mahomet to be infidels, and they say that it is right to hunt them. They are proud of taking Christian vessels, and of selling Christians as slaves.

There are some valuable plants in Malacca. There is one which has a seed called "pepper." There is a tree which has in the stem a pith called sago. Who collects the pepper and the sago? There are mines of tin. Who digs up the tin? The idle Malays will not take so much trouble, so the industrious Chinese labor instead. The Chinese come over by thousands to get rich in Malacca. As there is not room for them in their own country, they are glad to settle in other countries. But though the Chinese set an example of *industry*, they do not set an example of *goodness;* for they gamble, and so lose their *money*, they smoke opium, and so lose their *health*, and they commit many kinds of wickedness by which they lose their *souls*.

As for the Malays, they are so very idle, that when trees fall over the river, and block up the way, they will not be at the trouble of cutting a way through for their boats,—but will sooner creep *under* or climb *over* the fallen trees.

The capital of Malacca is Malacca, and this city belongs to the English; but it is of little use to them, because the harbor is not good.

SINGAPORE.

This city also belongs to the English, and it is of great use to them, because the harbor is one of the best in the world. Many ships come there to buy, and to sell, and amongst the rest, the Chinese junks. The city is built on a small island, very near the coast. There are many beautiful country houses perched on the hills, where English families live, and there are long flights of stone steps leading from their houses to the sea.

But many of the Malays have no home but a boat, hardly large enough to lie down in. There they gain a living by catching fish, and collecting shells, and coral, to exchange for sago, which is their food. These men are called "Ourang-lout," which means "Man of the water." Does not this name remind you of the apes called "Ourang-outang," which means "Man of the woods?" There are Ourang-outangs in the forests of Malacca, and they are more like men, and are more easily tamed than any other ape. Yet still how different is the *tamest* ape from the *wildest* man; for the one has an immortal soul, and the other has none.

The Malay language is said to be the easiest in the world, even as the Chinese is the most difficult. The Malay language has no cases or genders, or conjugations, which puzzle little boys so much in their Latin Grammars. It is easy for missionaries to learn the Malay language. When they know it, they can talk to the Chinese in Malacca in this language.

I will tell you of a school that an English lady has opened at Singapore for poor Chinese girls.

THE CHRISTIAN SCHOOL-GIRLS.

The two elder girls were sisters, and were called Chun and Han. Both of them, when they heard about Jesus, believed in him, and loved him. Yet their characters were very different, Chun being of a joyful disposition, and Han of a mournful and timid temper. They had no father, and their mother was employed in the school to take care of the little children, and to teach them needle-work; but she was a heathen.

When Chun and Han had been three years in the school, their mother wanted them to leave, and to come with her to her home. The girls were grieved at the thought of leaving their Christian teacher, and of living in a heathen home; yet they felt it was their duty to do as their mother wished. But they were anxious to be baptized before they went, if they could obtain their mother's consent. Their kind teacher, Miss Grant, thought it would be of no use to ask leave *long* before the time, lest the mother should carry her girls away, and lock them up. So she waited till the very evening fixed for the baptism. Miss Grant had been praying all day for help from God, and the two sisters had been praying together; and now the bell began to ring for evening service. Now the time was come when the mother must be asked.

"Do you know," said Miss Grant to the mother, "that the children are going to church with me?" "Yes," replied the mother, "wherever Missie pleases to take them." Then the lady told her of the baptism, and entreated her consent. At last the heathen mother replied, "If you wish it, I will not oppose you." Miss Grant, afraid lest the mother should change her mind, hastened into her palanquin, and the sisters hastened into theirs. Looking back, the lady perceived the mother was standing watching the palanquins. Seeing this, she stopped, saying, "Nomis, why should not you come, and see what is done?" To the lady's surprise, the mother immediately consented to come; and so this heathen mother was present at the baptism of her daughters. Their teacher, (who was their *mother in Christ,*) rejoiced with exceeding joy to see her dear girls give themselves to the Lord, and to hear them answer in their broken English, "All *dis* I do steadfastly believe."

Soon after their baptism, the girls went to live in their mother's house. To comfort them, Miss Grant promised to fetch them every Sunday, to spend the day with her. She came for them at five o'clock in the morning, before it was light, and took them back at nine, when it was quite dark. If she had not fetched them herself, they would not have been allowed to go.

After awhile, they were *not* allowed to go. The reason was, that the heathen mother wanted Chun to marry a heathen Chinaman. Chun refused to commit such a sin. Then her mother was angry, mocked her, and prevented her going to see Miss Grant. Still Chun refused. She saw her mother embroidering her wedding-dresses, but she still persisted that she would not marry a heathen, especially as she would have to bow down before an idol at her marriage. Chun grew very unhappy, and looked very pale, she wrote many letters to her kind friend, and offered up many prayers to her merciful God. And did the Lord hear her, and did He deliver her? He did. A Christian Chinaman, who had been brought up by a missionary, neard of Chun, and asked permission to marry her. He had never seen her, for it is not the custom in China for girls to be seen.

Miss Grant was delighted at the thought of her darling Chun marrying a Christian, and she helped to prepare for the wedding. There was no bowing down before an idol at that wedding, but an English clergymen read the service. Chun's face, according to the custom, was covered with a thick veil, and even her hands and feet were hidden. A few days after the wedding, Miss Grant, according to the custom, called on the newly married. She found the room beautifully ornamented, like all Chinese rooms at such times, but there were two ornaments seldom seen in China—two Bibles lying open on the table.

Chun long rejoiced that she had so firmly refused

to marry a heathen. One day, Miss Grant said to her, playfully, "Has your husband beaten you yet?" (for she knew that Chinamen think nothing of beating their wives.) Chun replied, with a sweet look, "O no! he often tells me, that *first* he thanks God, and then *you*, Miss, for having given me to him as his wife."

There was another girl at Miss Grant's school, named Been. Sometimes she was called Beneo, which means Miss Been, just as Chuneo means Miss Chun. Miss Grant hoped that Been loved the Saviour, and hated idols, but she soon lost her, for her parents took her to their heathen home.

After Been had been home a short time her mother died. The neighbors were astonished to find that Been refused to worship her mother's spirit, and to burn gold paper, to supply her with money in the other world. While her relations were busily occupied in their heathen ceremonies, Been sat silent and alone. Soon afterwards, her father, who cared not for her, sold her to a Chinaman to be his wife, for forty dollars.

Miss Grant heard her sad fate, and often longed to see her, but did not know where to find her. One evening, as she was paying visits in her palanquin, she saw a pair of bright black eyes looking through a hedge, and she felt sure that they were her own

Been's. She stopped, and calling the girl, saluted her affectionately. She was glad she had found out where Been lived, as she would now be able to pay her a visit.

Soon she called upon her, in her own dwelling;—a poor little hut in the midst of a sugar plantation. She brought as a present, a New Testament in English, and in large print. Been appeared delighted.

"Do you remember how to read it?" inquired Miss Grant.

"Yes, how could I forget?" Been sweetly replied.

"Well then, read," said Miss Grant.

Been read, "I am the good shepherd, and know my sheep."

"Do you understand?" inquired the lady.

"Yes," said Been, and she translated the words into Malay.

As Miss Grant was rising to depart, she observed a hen gathering her brood under her wings.

"Of what does that remind you, Been?"

"I know," said the poor girl; "I remember what I learnt at school;" and then in her broken English, she repeated the words: "As a hen *gaderet* her chickens under her wings, so would I have *gaderd de*, but *dou* wouldest not."

At this moment, Been's husband came in. The

girl was glad, for she wanted Miss Grant to ask him as a great favor, to allow her to spend next Sunday at the school. The husband consented. There was a joyful meeting indeed, on that Sunday, between Been, and Chun, and Han; nor was their affectionate teacher the least joyful of the company.

Siberia.

THIS is a name which makes people *shiver*, because it reminds them of the cold. It is a name which makes the Russians *tremble*, because it reminds them of banishment, for the emperor often sends those who offend him to live in Siberia.

Yet Siberia is not an ugly country, such as Tartary. It is not one dead flat, but it contains mountains, and forests, and rivers. Neither is Siberia a country in which nothing will grow; in some parts there is wheat, and where *wheat* will not grow *barley* will, and where *barley* will not grow *turnips* will. Yet there are not many cornfields in Siberia, for very few people live there. In the woods you will find blackberries, and wild roses, like those in England; and *red* berries, as well as *black* berries, and *lilies* as well as *roses*.

Still it must be owned that Siberia is a very cold country; for the snow is not melted till June, and it begins to fall again in September; so there are only two whole months without snow; they are July and August.

Inhabitants.—The Russians are the masters of Siberia, and they have built several large towns there. But these towns are very far apart, and there are many wild tribes wandering about the country.

One of these tribes is the Ostyaks. Their houses are in the shape of boxes, for they are square with flat roofs. There is a door, but you must stoop low to get in at it, unless you are a very little child; and there is a window with fish-skin instead of light. There is a chimney, too, and a blazing fire of logs in a hole in the ground. There is a trough, too, instead of a dining-table, and out of it the whole family eat, and even the dogs sometimes. The house is not divided into rooms, but into stalls, like those of a stable; and deer-skins are spread in the stalls, and they are the beds; each person sits and sleeps in his own stall, on his own deer-skin, except when the family gather round the fire, and sitting on low stools, warm themselves, and talk together.

In one of these snug corners, an old woman was seen, quite blind, yet sewing all day, and threading her needle by the help of her tongue. She wore a veil of thick cloth over her head, as all the Ostyak women do, and as she did not need light, she hid her head completely under it.

But though the Ostyaks are poor, they possess a

great treasure in their dogs, for these creatures are as useful as horses, and much more sensible. They need no whip to make them go, and no bridle to turn them the right way; it is enough to *tell* them when to set out, and to stop, or to turn, to move faster, or more slowly. These dogs are white, spotted with black; the hair on their bodies is short, but long on their handsome curling tails. They draw their masters in sledges, and are yoked in pairs. There are some large sledges, in which a man can lie down in comfort: to draw such a sledge twelve dogs are necessary; but there are small sledges in which a poor Ostyak can just manage to crouch, and two dogs can draw it. When the dogs are to be harnessed, they are not caught, as horses are, but only called. Yet they do not like work better than horses like it, and when they first set out they howl, but grow quiet after a little while.

The driver is sometimes cruel to these poor dogs, and corrects them for the smallest fault, by throwing a stone at them, or the great club he holds in his hand, or at least a snow-ball: if a hungry dog but stoop down to pick up a morsel of food on the road, he is punished in this manner. Yet it must be owned, that the dogs have their faults; they are greedy, and inclined to thieving. To keep food out of their way, the Ostyaks build store-houses, on the tops of very nigh poles. The dogs are always on the watch to slip into their master's houses. If the door be left open ever so little, a dog will squeeze in, if he can; but he does not stay *long* within, for he is soon thrust out with blows and kicks; the women scream at the sight of a dog in the hut, for they fear lest he will find the fish-trough. Yet after long journeys, the dogs are brought into the hut, and permitted to lie down by the fire, and to eat out of the family trough. At other times they sleep in the snow, and eat whatever is thrown to them. When they travel, bags of dried fish are brought in their sledges, to feed them by the way. The puppies are tenderly treated, and petted by the fire; yet many are killed for the sake of their fleecy hair, which is considered a fine ornament for pelisses.

The Ostyaks have another, and a greater treasure than dogs; they have reindeer. Those who live by fishing have dogs only, but those who dwell among the hills, have deer as well as dogs. Reindeer are like dogs in one respect, they can be driven without either a whip or a bit, which are so necessary for horses. But though they do not need the lashing of a whip, they require to be gently poked with a long pole; and though they do not need a bit, they require to be guided by a rein, fastened to their heads; because they are not like dogs, so sensible as to be managed by speaking.

But deer are very gentle, and are much more easily driven than horses. To drive horses four-in-hand is very difficult, but to drive four reindeer is not. The four deer are harnessed to the sledge all in a row, and a rein is fastened to the head of one; when *he* turns all the rest turn with him. Usually they trot, but they *can* gallop very fast, even down hill. When they are out of breath the driver lets them stop, and then the pretty creatures lie down, and cool their mouths with the snow lying on the ground.

Men ride upon reindeer; not upon their *backs*, but on their *necks;* for their backs are weak, while their necks are strong. Riders do not mount reindeer as they do horses,—by resting on their backs, and then making a spring, for that would hurt the poor animals; they lean on a long staff, and by its help, spring on the deer's neck. But it is not easy, when seated, to keep on; *you* would certainly fall off, for all strangers do, when they try to ride for the *first* time. The Ostyak knows how to keep his balance, by waving his long staff in the air, while the deer trots briskly along. But these reindeer have some curious fancies; they will not eat any food but such as they pluck themselves from the ground. It would be of no use at the end of a long journey, to put them in a stable;—they would not eat; they must be let loose to find their own nourishment, which is a kind of moss that grows wild among the hills.

The reindeer, after he is dead, is of as mnch use to the Ostyak, as when he was alive; for his skin is his master's clothing. Both men and women dress alike, in a suit that covers them from head to foot; the seams are well joined with thread, made of reindeer sinews, and the cold is kept well out. The Ostyak lets no part of his body be uncovered but just his face, and that would freeze, if he were not to rub it often with his hands, covered over with hairy reindeer gloves. The women cover their faces with thick veils. The Ostyak wears a great-coat made of the skin of a white deer; this gives him the appearance of a great white bear. He carries in his hand a bow taller than himself. His arrows are very long, and made of wood, pointed with iron. With these he shoots the wild animals. He is very glad when he can shoot a sable; because the Russian emperor requires every Ostyak to give him yearly, as a tax, the skins of two sables. The fur of the sable is very valuable, and is made into muffs and tippets, and pelisses for the Russian nobles.

But without his snow-shoes, the Ostyak would not

be able to pursue the wild animals, for he would sink in the snow. These shoes are made of long boards, turned up at the end like a boat, and fastened to the feet. What a wild creature an Ostyak must look, when he is hunting his prey, wrapped in his shaggy white coat,—his long dark hair floating in the wind, —his enormous bow in his hand, and his enormous shoes on his feet!

What is the character of this wild man? Ask what is his religion, and that will show you how foolish and fierce a creature he must be. The Ostyak says, that he believes in ONE God who cannot be seen, but he does not worship him *alone;* he worships other gods. And such gods! Dead men! When a man dies, his relations make a wooden image of him, and worship it for three years, and then bury it. But when a *priest* dies, his wooden image is worshipped *more* than three years; sometimes it is *never* buried; for the priests who are alive, encourage the people to go on worshipping dead priests' images, that they may get the offerings which are made to them.

But what do you think of men worshipping DEAD BEASTS? Yet this is what the Ostyaks do. When they have killed a wolf or a bear, they stuff its skin with hay, and gather round to mock it, to kick it, to spit upon it, and then—they stick it up on its hind legs in a corner of the hut, and WORSHIP it! Alas! how has Satan blinded their mind!

And in what manner do they worship the beasts? With screaming,—with dancing,—with swinging their swords,—by making offerings of fur, of silver and gold, and of reindeer. These reindeer they kill very cruelly, by stabbing them in various parts of their bodies, to please the cruel gods, or rather cruel devils whom they worship.

Has no one tried to convert the Ostyaks to God? The emperor of Russia will not allow protestant missionaries to teach in Siberia. He wishes the Ostyaks to belong to the Greek church, and he has tried to bribe them with presents of cloth to be baptized; and a good many have been baptized. But what good can such baptisms do to the soul?

The Russians do much harm to their subjects, by tempting them to buy brandy. There is nothing which the Ostyaks are so eager to obtain, as this dangerous drink. On one occasion, a traveller was surrounded by a troop of Ostyaks, all begging for brandy, and when they could get none, they brought a large heap of frozen fish, and laid it at the traveller's feet, saying, "Noble sir, we present you with this." They did get some brandy in return. Then, hoping for more, they brought a great salmon, and a sturgeon, as long as a man. They seemed ready to part with all they had, for the sake of brandy.

Thus you see how much harm the Ostyaks have learned from their acquaintance with the Russians. The chief good they have got, has been learning to build houses; for once they lived only intents.

THE SAMOYEDES.

This tribe lives so far to the north, that they see very little of the Russians, though they belong to the emperor of Russia. They live close by the Northern Sea. Imagine how very cold it must be. The Samoyedes inhabit tents made of reindeer skins, such as the Ostyaks used to live in. They are a much wilder people than the Ostyaks. The women dress in a strange fantastic manner; not contented with a reindeer dress, as the Ostyaks are, they join furs and skins of various sorts together; and instead of veiling their faces, they wear a gay fur hat, with lappets; and at the back of their necks a glutton's tail hangs down, as well as long tails of their own hair, with brass rings jingling together at the end.

But if their taste in *dress* is laughable, their taste in *food*, is horrible, as you will see. A traveller went with a Samoyede family for a little while. They were drawn by reindeer, in sledges, and other reindeer followed of their own accord. When they stopped for the night, they pitched the tent, covering the long poles with their reindeer skins, sewed together. The snow covered the ground inside the tent, but no one thought of sweeping it away. It was easy to get water to fill the kettle, as a few lumps of snow soon melted. Some of the men slept by the blazing fire, while others went out, armed with long poles, to defend the deer from the wolves. There was in the party a child of two years old, with its mother. The child was allowed to help himself to porridge out of the great kettle. The traveller offered him white sugar; but at first he called it snow, and threw it away; soon, however, he learned to like it, and asked for some whenever he saw the stranger at tea. At night, the child was laid in a long basket, and was closely covered with furs; in the same basket also, he travelled in the sledge.

One day the traveller saw a Samoyede feast. A reindeer was brought, and killed before the tent door; and its bleeding body was taken into the tent, and devoured, all raw as it was, with the heartiest appetite. It was dreadful to see the Samoyedes gnawing the flesh off the bones; their faces all stained with blood, and even the child had his share of the raw meat. Truly they looked more like wolves than men.

I might go on to tell you of many other tribes; but I must be content just to mention a few.

There is a tribe who live in the eastern part of Siberia, called the Yakuts, and instead of deer, and dogs, they keep horses, and oxen, and strange to say, they *ride* upon the oxen; and *eat* the horses. A horse's head is counted by them a most dainty dish. The cows live in one room, and the family live in the next, with the calves, which are tied to posts by the fire, and enjoy the full blaze. You may suppose that the calves need the warmth of the fire, when I tell you that the windows of the house are made of ice, but that the cold is so great, that the ice does not melt.

There is a large tribe called the Buraets. They dwell in tents. They are Buddhists. At one time the Russians allowed missionaries to go to them. There was an old man named Andang, who used to attend the services very regularly. His wife accompanied him. One Sunday the preacher spoke much of heaven and its glories. The old woman, on returning to her tent, said to her husband, "Old man, I am going home to-night." Her husband did not understand her meaning: then she said, "I love Jesus

Christ, and I think I shall be with him to-night." She lay down in her tent that night, but rose no more. In the morning, the old man found her stiff and cold. He saddled his horse, and set off to tell the missionary. "O sir," said he, with tears, "my wife is gone home." When the missionary heard the account of her death, he felt cheered by the hope that the old woman, though born a heathen, had died a Christian, and had left her tent to dwell in a glorious mansion above; for how was it that she felt no fear of death, and how was it that she felt heaven was her home? Was it not because Jesus loved her, and because she loved Jesus?

THE BANISHED RUSSIANS.

Siberia is the land to which the emperor sends many of his people, when they displease him. In passing through Siberia, you would often see wagons full of women, children, and old men, followed by a troop of young men, and guarded by a band of soldiers on horseback. You might know them to be the banished Russians. What is to become of them? Some are to work in the mines, and some are to work in the factories. Some are to have a less heavy punishment; they are to be set free, in the midst of Siberia, to support themselves in any way they can. Gentlemen and ladies have a small sum of money allowed them by the emperor, and they live in the towns.

These people are called in Siberai, "the unfortunates." Some of them have not deserved to be banished; but some have been guilty of crimes.

CITIES.

There are a few cities in Siberia, but only a few, and they have been built by the Russians.

The three chief cities are,—

Tobolsk, on the west, on the river Oby.

Irkutsk, in the midst, on the lake Baikal.

Yarkutsk, on the east, on the river Lena.

OF THESE CITIES,

Tobolsk is the handsomest.

Irkutsk is the pleasantest.

Yarkutsk is the coldest.

It is not surprising that Tobolsk should be the handsomest, for there the governor of Siberia resides.

A great many Chinese come to Irkutsk to trade, and they bring quantities of tea.

Yarkutsk is the coldest town in the world; there may be others nearer the north, but none lie exposed to such cold winds. The inhabitants scarcely dare admit the light, for fear of increasing the cold; and they make only one or two very small windows in their houses. Yet in summer vegetables grow freely in the gardens.

The Ostyaks live near the Oby.
The Buraets live near lake Baikal.
The Yakuts live near the Lena.

THE URAL MOUNTAINS.

They are full of treasures; gold, silver, iron, copper, and precious stones. They are dug up by the banished Russians, and sent in great wagons to Russia, to increase the riches of the emperor.

Kamkatka.

It is impossible to look at Siberia, without being struck with the shape of Kamkatka, which juts out like a short arm. It is a peninsula. A beautiful country it is; full of mountains, and rivers, and woods, and waterfalls, and not as cold as might be expected. But there are not many people dwelling in it; for though it is larger than Great Britain, all the inhabitants might be contained in one of our small towns. And why are there so few in so fine a country? Because the people love brandy better than labor. They have been corrupted by the Russian soldiers, and traders, and convicts, and they are sickening and dying away.

A traveller once said to a Kamkatdale, "How should you like to see a ship arrive here from China, laden with tea and sugar?" "I should like it well," replied the man, "but there is one thing I should like better—to see a ship arrive full of *men;* it is men we want, for our men are sick; of the twelve here, six are too weak to hunt or fish."

But the ship that would do the most good to Kamkatka, is a missionary ship. The Greek church is the religion; but *no* religion is much thought of in Kamkatka; hunting and fishing only are cared for. Yet I fear if missionaries were to go to Kamkatka, the emperor of Russia would send them away.

Where there are few men, there are generally many beasts and birds; this is the case in Kamkatka.

One of the most curious animals in Siberia, is the Argalis, or mountain sheep. It is remarkable for its enormous horns, curled in a very curious manner. Think not it is like one of our quiet, foolish sheep; there is no animal at once so strong and so active. It is such a climber, that no wolf or bear can follow it to the high places, hanging over awful precipices, where it walks as firmly as you do upon the pavement. Sometimes a hunter finds it among the mountains, and just as he is going to shoot it, the creature disappears:—it has thrown itself down a precipice! Is it dashed to pieces? No, it fell unhurt, and has escaped without a bruise; for its bones are very strong, and its skin very thick.

The bears of Kamkatka live chiefly upon fish and berries, and seldom attack men. Yet men hunt them for their skins, and for their fat. The skins make cloaks, and the fat is used for lamps; but their flesh is thrown to the dogs. Many of the bears are very thin. It is only *fat* bears that can sleep all the winter in their dens without food; *thin* bears cannot sleep long, and even in winter they prowl about for food. Dogs are very much afraid of them. A large party of travellers, who were riding in sledges, drawn by dogs, observed the dogs suddenly begin to snuff the air, and lo! immediately afterwards, a bear at full speed crossed the road, and ran towards a forest. Great confusion took place among the dogs; they set off with all their might; some broke their harness, others got entangled among the trees, and overturned their sledges. But the bear did not escape; for the travellers shot him through the leg, and afterwards through the body; and the dogs feasted on *his* flesh, instead of the bear feasting on *theirs*.

Hunting seals is one of the occupations of the Kamkatdales. Three men in sledges, each sledge drawn by five dogs, once got upon a large piece of ice, near the shore. They had killed two seals upon the ice, when they suddenly perceived that the ice was moving, and carrying them out to sea. They were already too far from land, to be able to get back. They knew not what would become of them, and much they feared they should perish from cold and hunger. The ice was so slippery that they were in great danger of sliding into the sea. To prevent this, they stuck their long poles deep into the ice, and tied themselves to the poles. They were driven about for many days; but one morning,—to their great joy, they found they were close to the shore. They did not forget to praise God for so mercifully saving their lives; though they were so weak from want of food, as scarcely to be able to creep ashore.

CHARACTER.—The Kamkatdales are generous and grateful. A poor family will sometimes receive another family into the house for six weeks; and when the food is nearly gone, the generous host, not liking to tell his visitors of it, serves up a dish of different sorts of meat and vegetables, mixed together; the visitors know this is a sign that the food is almost exhausted, and they take their leave.

Did I say the Kamkatdales are grateful? I will give you an instance of their gratitude. A traveller met a poor boy. He remembered his face, and said, "I think I have seen you before." "You have," said the boy; "I rowed you down the river last summer, and you were so kind as to give me a skin, and some flints; and now I have brought the skin of a sable as a present for you." The traveller, perceiving the boy had no shirt, and that his skin dress was tattered, refused the present; but seeing the boy was going away in tears, he called him back, and accepted it. A Chinese servant, who was standing by, pitied so much the ragged condition of the boy, that he gave him one of his own thin nankin shirts.

Thibet.

I CANNOT tell you much about Thibet; and the reason is, that so few travellers have been there. And why have so few been there? Is it because the mountains are so steep and high, the paths so narrow and dangerous? All this is true; but it is not mountains that keep travellers out of Thibet; it is the Chinese government; for Thibet belongs to China, and you know how carefully the emperor of China keeps strangers out of his empire.

How did the Chinese get possession of Thibet? A long while ago, a Hindoo army invaded the land, and the people in their fright sent to China for help. The Chinese came, drove away the Hindoos, and stayed themselves. They are not hard masters, they govern very mildly; only they require a sum of money to be sent every year to Pekin, as tribute.

But though Thibet belongs to China, the Chinese language is not spoken there.

The people are like the Tartars in appearance; they

have the same bony face, sharp black eye, and straight black hair; but a much fresher complexion, owing to the fresh mountain air they breathe.

The Himalaya mountains, the highest in Asia, lie between Thibet and Hindostan. Their peaks are always covered with snow, and rapid streams pour down the rugged sides. The snow on the mountain-tops makes Thibet very cold; but there are warm valleys where grapes, and even rice flourish.

The people build their houses in the warmest spots they can find; they try to find a place sheltered from the north wind, by a high rock, and lying open to the south sun. Their dwellings are only made of stones, heaped together, and the roofs are flat. Their riches consist in flocks of sheep and goats. They have, another animal, which is not known in England, and yet a very useful creature, because, like a cow, it yields rich milk, and like a horse, it carries burdens. This animal is called the Yak, and resembles both a horse and a cow. Its chief beauty is its tail, which is much finer than a horse's tail, and is black, and glossy, soft and flowing. Many of these tails are sent to India, where they are used as fly-flappers.

The sheep and goats of Thibet are more useful than ours; for they are taught to carry burdens over the mountains. They may be seen following each other in long trains, with large packs fastened on their little backs, and climbing up very narrow and steep paths.

And what is in these packs? Wool: not sheep's wool, but goat's wool: for the goats of Thibet have very fine wool under their hair. No such wool is found on any other goats. But though the people of Thibet can weave common cloth, they cannot weave this beautiful wool, as it deserves to be woven. Therefore they send it to a country the other side of the Himalaya mountains, called Cashmere; and there it is woven into the most beautiful shawls in all the world.

But wool is not the only riches of Thibet. There is gold to be found there; some in large pieces, and some in small dust. There are also large mines of copper. And what use is made of these riches? The worst in the world. With the gold and copper many IDOLS are made; for Thibet is a land of idols. The religion is the same there as in China,—the Buddhist;—and that is a religion of idols.

But there is an idol in Thibet, which there is not in China. It is a LIVING IDOL. He is called the Grand Lama. There are Lamas in Tartary, but the GRAND Lama is in Thibet. He is looked up to as the greatest being in the world, by all the Lamas in Tartary, and by all the people of the Buddhist religion. There are more people,—a *great many* more,—who honor *him*, than who honor our GREAT GOD.

But this man leads a miserable life. When one Lama dies, another is chosen;—some little baby,—and he is placed in a very grand palace, and worshipped as a god all his life long. I have heard of one of these baby Lamas, who, when only eighteen months old, sat up with great majesty on his pile of cushions. When strangers entered, he looked at them kindly, and when they made a speech to him, he bowed his little head very graciously. What a sad fate for this poor infant! To be set up as a god, and taught to think himself a god—while all the time he is a helpless, foolish, sinful, dying creature!

LASSA.

This is the chief city of Thibet. Here is the palace of the Grand Lama. It is of enormous size. What do you think of TEN THOUSAND rooms? Did you ever hear of so *large* a house? Neither did you ever hear of so *high* a house. It is almost as high as the pinnacle of St. Paul's church. There are seven stories, and on the highest story are the state apartments of the Grand Lama. It is no matter to him how many flights of stairs there may be to reach his rooms; for he is never allowed to walk; but it is fatiguing for his worshippers to ascend so high. I suppose the priests make their Grand Lama live so high up, that he may be like our God who dwells in the highest heavens. Who occupy the ten thousand rooms of the palace? Chiefly idols of gold and silver. The house outside is richly adorned, and its roof glitters with gold.

There are many magnificent houses in Thibet, where priests live. No one could live with them, who could not bear a great noise: for three times a day the priests meet to worship, and each time they hollo with all their might, to do honor to Buddha. The noise is stunning, but they do not think it loud enough; so on feast days, they use copper instruments, such as drums and trumpets, of the most enormous size, and with them they send forth an overwhelming sound.

This unmeaning noise may well remind us of a sound—louder far—that shall one day be heard; so loud that *all the world* will hear it. It is the sound of the LAST TRUMPET! It will wake the dead. Stout hearts will quail; devils will tremble; but all those who love the Lord, will rejoice and say, "Lo, this is our God; we have waited for Him, and He will save us."—(Is. xxv. 9.)

Ceylon.

THIS is one of the most beautiful islands in the world. Part of it indeed is flat—that part near Hindostan; but in the midst—there are mountains; and streams running down their sides, and swelling into lovely rivers, winding along the fruitful valleys. Such scenes might remind you of Switzerland, the most beautiful country in Europe.

The chief beauty of Ceylon is her TREES.

I will mention a few of the beautiful, curious, and useful trees of this delightful island. The tree for which Ceylon is celebrated, is the CINNAMON tree. For sixty miles along the shore, there are cinnamon groves, and the sweet scent may be perceived far off upon the seas. If you were to see a cinnamon-tree, you might mistake it for a laurel;—a tree so often found in English gardens. The cinnamon-trees are never allowed to grow tall, because it is only the upper branches which are much prized for their bark. The little children of Ceylon may often be seen sitting in the shade, peeling off the bark with their knives; and this bark is afterwards sent to England to flavor puddings, and to mix with medicine.

There are also groves of cocoa-nut trees on the shores of Ceylon. A few of these trees are a little fortune to a poor man; for he can eat the *fruit*, build his house with the *wood*, roof it with the *leaves*, make cups of the *shell*, and use the oil of the *kernel* instead of candles.

The JACK-TREE bears a larger fruit than any other in the world;—as large as a horse's head,—and so heavy that a woman can only carry one upon her head to market. This large fruit does not hang on the tree by a stalk, but grows out of the trunk, or the great branches. This is well arranged, for so large a fruit would be too heavy for a stalk, and might fall off, and hurt the heads of those sitting beneath its shade. The outside of this fruit is like a horse-chestnut, green, and prickly; the inside is yellow, and is full of kernels, like beans. The wood is like mahogany,—hard and handsome.

But there is a tree in Ceylon, still more curious than the jack-tree. It is the TALPOT-TREE. This is a very tall tree, and its top is covered by a cluster of round leaves, each leaf so large, that it would do for a carpet, for a common-sized room; and one single

LEAF, cut it in three-cornered pieces, will make a TENT! When cut up, the leaves are used for fans and books. But this tree bears no fruit till just before it dies,— that is till it is *fifty* years old: THEN—an enormous bud is seen, rearing its huge head in the midst of the crown of leaves;—the bud bursts with a loud noise, and a yellow flower appears,—a flower so large, that it would fill a room! The flower turns into fruit. THAT SAME YEAR THE TREE DIES!

PEOPLE.—And who are the people who live in this beautiful land?

In the flat part of the island, towards the north, the people resemble the Hindoos, and speak and think like them; and they are called Tamuls.

But among the mountains of the south a different kind of people live, called the Cingalese. They do not speak the Tamul language, nor do they follow the Hindoo religion. They follow the Buddhist religion. You know this is the religion of the greater part of the nations. Ceylon is full of the temples of Buddha. In each temple there is an inner dark room, very large, where Buddha's image is kept,—a great image that almost fills the room.

The priests in their yellow cloaks, with their shaven heads and bare feet, may be seen every morning begging from door to door; but *proud* beggars they

DEVIL PRIESTS. p. 265

are,—not condescending to *speak*,—but only standing with their baskets ready to receive rice and fruit; and the only thanks they give—are their blessings.

There is another worship in Ceylon, and it is more followed than the worship of Buddha, yet it is the most horrible that you can imagine. It is the worship of the DEVIL! Buddha taught, when he was alive, that there was no God, but that there were many devils: yet he forbid people to worship these devils; but no one minds what he said on that point.

There are many *devil priests*. When any one is sick, it is supposed that the devil has caused the sickness, and a devil priest is sent for. And what can the priest do? He dances,—he sings,—with his face painted,—small bells upon his legs,—and a flaming torch in each hand; while another man beats a loud drum. He dances, he sings—all night long,—sometimes changing his white jacket for a black, or his black for a white,—sometimes falling down, and sometimes jumping up,—sometimes reeling, and sometimes running,—and all this he does to please the devil, and to coax him to come out of the sick person. This is what he *pretends*;—but in *reality*, he seeks to get money by his tricks. The people are very fond of these devil-dancers; it *tires* them to listen to the Buddhist priests, mumbling out of their books, the five hundred and fifty histories of Buddha; but it *delights* them to watch all night the antics of a devil priest.

What is the character of these deceived people? They are polite, and obliging, but as deceitful as their own priests. They are not even *sincere* in their wrong religion, but are ready to *pretend* to be of any religion which is most convenient. The Portuguese once were masters of Ceylon, and they tried to make the people Roman Catholics. Then the Dutch came, who tried to force them to be Protestants. Many infants were baptized, who grew up to be heathen priests. Now the English are masters of Ceylon; they do not *oblige* the people to be Christians, yet many pretend to be Christians who are not.

A man was once asked, "Are you a Buddhist?"

"No," he replied.

"Are you a Mahomedan?"

"No."

"Are you a Roman Catholic?"

"No."

"What is your religion?"

"Government religion."

Such was his answer. This man had no religion at all,—he only wished to obtain the favor of the governor. But will he obtain the favor of the Governor of the world, the King of kings?

We have said nothing yet about the appearance of the Cingalese. Both men and women wear a piece of cloth wound round their waists, called a comboy; but they do not, like the Hindoos, twist it over their shoulders; they wear a jacket instead. Neither do the men wear turbans, as in India, but they fasten their hair with a comb, while the women fasten theirs with long pins. The Cingalese ladies and gentlemen imitate the English dress, especially when they come to a party at the English Governor's house. Then they wear shoes and stockings instead of sandals; the gentlemen contrive to place a hat over their long hair, by first taking out the combs; yet they still wind a comboy over their English clothes. The Hindoos do not thus imitate the English, for they are too proud of their own customs. Hindoo ladies never go into company; but Cingalese ladies may be seen at parties, arrayed in colored satin jackets, and adorned with golden hair-pins, and diamond necklaces.

You have heard of the foolish ideas the Hindoos entertain about castes. It is the Brahmin priests who teach *them* these opinions. The Buddhist priests say nothing about castes; yet the Cingalese have castes of their *own;* but not the *same* castes as the

Hindoos. There are twenty-one castes in all; the highest caste consists of the husbandmen, and the lowest of the mat-weavers.

Below the lowest caste, are the OUTCASTS! The poor outcasts live in villages by themselves, hated by all. When they meet any one, who are not outcasts, they go as near to the hedge as they can, with their hands on the top of their heads, to show their respect. These poor creatures are accustomed to be treated as if they were dogs. What pride there is in man's heart! How is it one poor worm can lift himself up so high above his fellow-worm, though both are made of the same dust, and shall lie down in the same dust together!

KANDY.

This town is built among the high mountains. It was built there for the same reason that the eagle builds her nest on the top of a tall rock,—to get out of the reach of enemies. But the proud king, who once dwelt there, has been conquered, and now England's Queen rules over Ceylon. No wonder that the proud king had enemies, for he was a monster of cruelty. His palace is still to be seen. See that high tower, and that open gallery at the top! There the *last king* used to stand to enjoy the sight of his subjects' agonies. Those who had offended him were killed in the Court below,—killed not in a common manner, but in all kinds of barbarous ways,—such as by being cut in pieces, or by swallowing melted lead. At length the Cingalese invited the English to come and deliver them from their tyrant; the English came and shut him up in prison till he died, and now an English governor rules over Ceylon.

The greatest curiosity to be seen at Kandy is a TOOTH! a tooth that the people say was taken out of the mouth of their Buddha. It is kept in a splendid temple on a golden table, in a golden box of great size. There are seven boxes one inside the other, and in the innermost box, wrapped up in gold, there is a piece of ivory, the size of a man's thumb,—that is the tooth of Buddha! Every day it is worshipped, and offerings of fruit and flowers are presented.

COLOMBO.

This is the chief *English* town of Ceylon, as Kandy is the chief *Cingalese* town. The English governor lives here, but he has a house at Kandy too, where he may enjoy the cool mountain air. There is a fine road from Colombo to Kandy, broader and harder than English roads; yet it is out through steep mountains, and winds by dangerous precipices. But there are laborers in Ceylon stronger than any in England. I mean the ELEPHANTS. It is curious to see this huge animal meekly walking along with a plank across its tusks, or dragging wagons full of large stones. Among the mountains there are herds of *wild* elephants, sometimes a hundred may be seen in one herd. There are no elephants in the world as courageous as those of Ceylon, yet they are very obedient when tamed. If you wished to visit the mountains, you might safely ride upon the back of the sure-footed elephant, and all your brothers and sisters, however many, might ride with you.

MISSIONARIES.—There are some in Ceylon, and some of the heathens have obeyed their voice.

There was once a devil priest. Having been detected in some crime, he was imprisoned at Kandy, and while in prison he read a Christian tract, and was converted. Thus (like Onesimus, of whom we read in the Bible,) he escaped from *Satan's* prison, while shut up in *man's* prison. When he was set free, he was baptized by the missionary at Kandy, and he chose to be called Abraham. What name did he choose for his son, a boy of fourteen? Isaac. He buried his conjuring books, though he might have sold them for eight pounds. His cottage was in a village fifteen miles from Kandy. He had left it—a *wicked* man; he returned to it a *good* man.

After some time, a missionary went to visit Abraham in his cottage. A good Cingalese was his guide. The walk there was beautiful, along narrow paths, amidst fields of rice, through dark thickets, and long grass. No one in Abraham's village had ever seen the fair face of an Englishman; and the sight of the missionary alarmed the inhabitants. Abraham's family was the only Christian family in that place. How glad Abraham felt at the sight of the missionary,—almost as glad as the *first* Abraham felt at the sight of the three angels. When the missionary entered, Abraham was teaching his wife, for she was soon to be baptized. By what name? By the name of Sarah. There were seven children in the family. How hard it must be for Abraham to bring them up as Christians, in the midst of his heathen neighbors. Even his brothers hate him, wound his cattle, and break down his fences. Once they pointed a gun at him, but it did not go off. Abraham's comfort is to walk over to Kandy every Saturday, to worship God there on Sunday with the Christians; and he does not find fifteen miles too far for his willing feet. May the Lord preserve Abraham, faithful in the midst of the wicked.

Borneo.

This is the largest island in the world, except one. Borneo is of a different shape from our Britain, but if you could join Britain and Ireland in one, both together would not be as large as Borneo. Yet how unlike is Borneo to Britain! Britain is a Christian island. Borneo is a heathen island. Yet Borneo is not an island of *idols*, as Ceylon is. *All* heathens do not worship idols. I will tell you who live in Borneo, and you will see why there are so few idols there.

Many people have come from Malacca, and settled in Borneo; so the island is full of Malays. These people have a cunning and cruel look, and no wonder;—for many of them are PIRATES! It is a common custom in Borneo to go out in a large boat,—to watch for smaller boats,—to seize them—to bind the men in chains, and to bring them home as slaves. There are no seas in the world so dangerous to sail in, as the seas near Borneo, not only on account of the rocks, but on account of the great number of pirates. What is the religion of Borneo? It is Mahomedanism.

But the Malays do not follow the laws of Mahomet as the Turks do. They do not mind the hours of prayer, nor do they attend regularly at the mosque. This is not surprising, for they do not understand the Koran. Mahomet wrote in Arabic, and the Malays do not understand Arabic. Why do they not get the Koran translated? Mahomet did not wish the book to be translated. Why then do not the Malays learn Arabic? I wonder they do not, but I suppose they are too idle, and too careless. The boys go to school and learn to read and write their own easy language—the Malay; and they learn also to repeat whole chapters of the Koran, but without understanding a word. Still they think it a great advantage to know these chapters, because they imagine that by repeating them, they can drive away evil spirits.

The Malays observe Mahomet's law against eating pork; but many of them drink wine, though Mahomet forbids it. However, they follow Mahomet in not having dancing at their feasts; indeed, their behavior at feasts is sober and orderly, for they amuse themselves chiefly by singing, and repeating poems. They have only two meals a day, and they live chiefly upon rice, which they eat, sitting cross-legged on the floor. They get tea from China, and drink many cups during the day, in the same way as the Chinese.

The ladies are treated like the ladies of Turkey, and shut up in their houses, to spend their time in folly and idleness.

The men scarcely work at all, but employ the slaves they have stolen at sea, to labor in their fields. Their houses are not better than barns, and not nearly as strong; for the sides and roof are generally made only of large leaves. They are built upon posts, as in Siam. It is well to be out of the reach of the leeches, crawling on the ground.

The Malays dress in loose clothes, trowsers, and jacket, and broad sash; the women are wrapped in a loose garment, and wear their glossy black hair flowing over their shoulders. The rich men dress magnificently, and quite cover their jackets with gold, while the ladies delight to sparkle with jewels.

BRUNI.

This is the capital. It is often called Borneo, and it is written down in the maps by this name. It is one of the most curious cities in the world; for most of the houses are built in the river, and most of the streets are only water. Every morning a great market is held on the water. The people come in boats from all the country round, bringing fruit and vegetables to sell, and they paddle up and down the city till they have sold their goods.

The Sultan's palace is built upon the bank, close to the water; and the front of his palace is open; so that it is easy to come in a boat, and to gaze upon him, as he sits cross-legged on his throne, arrayed in purple satin, glittering with gold.

There is a mosque in Bruni; but it is built only of brick, and has nothing in it but a wooden pulpit; and hardly anybody goes there, though a man stands outside making a loud noise on a great drum, to invite people to come in.

THE DYAKS.

These are a savage people who inhabit Borneo. They lived there before the Malays came, and they have been obliged to submit to them. They are savages indeed. They are darker than the Malays; yet they are not black; their skin is only the color of copper. Their hair is cut short in front, but streams down their backs; their large mouths show a quantity of black teeth, made black by chewing the betel-nut. They wear very little clothing, but they adorn their ears, and arms, and legs, with numbers of brass rings. Their looks are wild and fierce, but not cunning like the looks of the Malays. They are not Mahomedans; they have hardly any religion at all. They believe there are some gods, but they know hardly anything about them, and they do not want to know. They neither make images to the gods, nor say prayers to them. They live like the beasts, thinking only of this life; yet they are more unhappy than beasts, for they imagine there are evil spirits among the woods and hills, watching to do them harm. It is often hard to persuade them to go to the top of a mountain, where they say evil spirits dwell. Such a people would be more ready to listen to a missionary than those who have idols, and temples, and priests, and sacred books.

Their wickedness is very great. It is their chief delight to get the heads of their enemies. There are a great many different tribes of Dyaks, and each tribe tries to cut off the heads of other tribes. The Dyaks who live by the sea are the most cruel; they go out in the boats to rob, and to bring home, not *slaves*, but HEADS! And how do they treat a head when they get it? They take out the brains, and then they dry it in the smoke, with the flesh and hair still on; then they put a string through it, and fasten it to their waists. The evening that they have got some new heads, the warriors dance with delight,—their heads dangling by their sides;—and they turn round in the dance, and gaze upon their heads,—and shout,—and yell with triumph! At night they still keep the heads near them; and in the day, they play with them, as children with their dolls, talking to them, putting food in their mouths, and the betel-nut between their ghastly lips. After wearing the heads many days, they hang them up to the ceilings of their rooms.

No English lord thinks so much of his pictures, as the Dyaks do of their heads. They think these heads are the finest ornaments of their houses. The man who has *most* heads, is considered the *greatest* man. A man who has NO HEADS is despised! If he wishes to be respected, he must get a head as soon as he can. Sometimes a man, in order to get a head, will go out to look for a poor fisherman, who has done him no harm, and will come back with his head.

When the Dyaks fight against their enemies, they try to get, not only the heads of *men*, but also the heads of *women* and CHILDREN. How dreadful it must be to see a poor BABY'S HEAD hanging from the ceiling! There was a Dyak who lost all his property by fire, but he cared not for losing anything, so much as for losing his PRECIOUS HEADS; nothing could console him for THIS loss; some of them he had cut off himself, and others had been cut off by his father, and left to him!

People who are so bent on killing, as these Dyaks are, must have many enemies. The Dyaks are always in fear of being attacked by their enemies. They are afraid of living in lonely cottages; they think it a better plan for a great many to live together, that they may be able to defend themselves, if surprised in the night. Four hundred Dyaks will live together in one house. The house is very large. To make it more safe, it is built upon *very high posts*, and there are ladders to get up by. The posts are sometimes forty feet high; so that when you are in the house, you find yourself as high as the tall trees. There is one very large room, where all the men and women sit, and talk, and do their work in the day. The women pound the rice, and weave the mats, while the men make weapons of war, and the little children play about. There is always much noise and confusion in this room. There are a great many doors along one side of the long room; and each of these doors leads into a small room where a family lives; the parents, the babies, and the girls sleep there, while the boys of the family sleep in the large room, that has just been described.

You know already what are the ornaments on which each family prides itself,—the HEADS hanging up in their rooms! It is the SEA Dyaks who live in these very large houses.

The HILL Dyaks do not live in houses quite so large. Yet several families inhabit the same house. In the midst of their villages, there is always one house where the boys sleep. In this house all the HEADS of the village are kept. The house is round, and built on posts, and the entrance is underneath through the floor. As this is the best house in the village, travellers are always brought to this house to sleep. Think how dreadful it must be, when you wake in the night to see thirty or forty horrible heads, dangling from the ceiling! The wind, too, which comes in through little doors in the roof, blows the heads about; so that they knock against each other, and seem almost as if they were still alive. This is the HEAD-HOUSE.

These Hill Dyaks do not often get a new head; but when they do, they come to the Head-House at night, and sing to the new head, while they beat upon their loud gongs. What do they say to the new head?

"Your head, and your spirit, are now ours. Persuade your countrymen to be slain by us. Let them wander in the fields, that we may bring the heads of your brethren, and hang them up with your heads."

How much Satan must delight in these prayers. They are prayers just suited to that great MURDERER and DESTROYER!

The Malays are enemies to all the Dyaks; and they have burnt many of their houses, cut down their fruit trees, and taken their children captives. The Dyaks complain bitterly of their sufferings. Some of them say, "We do not live like men, but like monkeys; we are hunted from place to place; we have no houses; and when we light a fire, we fear lest the smoke should make our enemies know where we are."

They say they live like monkeys. But why do they behave like tigers?

An English gentleman, named Sir James Brooke, has settled in Borneo, and has become a chief of a large tract of land. His house is near the river Sarawak. He has persuaded the Sultan of Borneo, to give the English a VERY LITTLE island called the Isle of Labuan. It is a desert island. Of what use can this small island be to England? English soldiers may live there, and try to prevent pirates infesting the seas. If it were not for the pirates, Borneo would be able to send many treasures to foreign countries. It is but a little way from Borneo to Singapore, and there are many English merchants at Singapore, ready to buy the precious things of Borneo. Gold is found in Borneo, mixed with the earth. But I don't know who would dig it up, if it were not for the industrious Chinese, who come over in great numbers to get money in this island. Diamonds are found there, and a valuable metal called antimony.

The sago-tree, the pepper plant, and the sugar-cane, and the cocoa-nut tree are abundant.

The greatest curiosity that Borneo possesses are the eatable nests. These white and transparent nests are found in the caves by the sea-shore, and they are the work of a little swallow. The Chinese give a high price for these nests, that they may make soup for their feasts.

ANIMALS.—Borneo has very few large animals. There are, indeed, enormous alligators in the rivers, but there are no lions or tigers; and even the bears are small, and content to climb the trees for fruit and honey. The majestic animal which is the pride of Ceylon, is not found in Borneo: I mean the elephant.

Yet the woods are filled with living creatures. Squirrels and monkeys sport among the trees. The leaps of the monkeys are amazing; hundreds will jump one after the other, from a tree as high as a house, and not one will miss his footing; yet now and then a monkey has a fall. The most curious kind of monkey is found in Borneo—the Ourang-outang; but it is one of the least active; it climbs carefully from branch to branch, always holding by its hands before it makes a spring. These Ourang-outangs are not as large as a man, yet they are much stronger. All the monkeys sleep in the trees; in a minute a monkey makes its bed by twisting a few branches together.

Beneath the trees—two sorts of animals, very unlike each other, roam about,—the clumsy hog, and the graceful deer. As the *largest* sort of *monkeys* is found in Borneo, so is the *smallest* sort of *deer*. There is a deer that has legs only eight inches long. There is no more elegant creature in the world than this bright eyed, swift-footed little deer.

Japan.

This is the name of a great empire. There are three principal islands. One of these is very long, and very narrow; it is about a thousand miles long,—much longer than Great Britain, but not nearly as broad. Yet the three islands *together* are larger than our island. There is a fourth island near the Japan islands, called Jesso, and it is filled with Japanese people.

You know it is difficult to get into China; but it is far more difficult to get into Japan. The emperor has boats always watching round the coast, to prevent strangers coming into his country. These boats are so made, that they cannot go far from the shore. No Japanese ship is ever seen floating in a foreign harbor. If it be difficult to get *into* Japan, it is also difficult to get *out* of her. There is a law condemning to *death* any Japanese who leaves his country. The Chinese also are forbidden to leave their land; but *they* do not mind their laws as well as the Japanese mind *theirs*.

I shall not be able to tell you much about Japan; as strangers may not go there, nor natives come from it. English ships very seldom go to Japan, because they are so closely watched. The guard-boats surround them night and day. When it is dark, lanterns are lighted, in order the better to observe the strangers. One English captain entreated permission to land, that he might observe the stars with his instruments, in order afterwards to make maps; but he could only get leave to land on a little island where there were a few fishermen's huts; and all the time he was there, the Japanese officers kept their eye upon him. He was told that he must not measure the land. It seems that the Japanese were afraid that his *measuring* the land would be the beginning of his taking it away. However, he had no such intention, and was content with measuring the SEA.

He asked the Japanese to sell him a supply of fruit and vegetables for his crew, and a supply was brought; but the Japanese would take no money in return. He wanted to buy bullocks, that his crew might have beef, but the Japanese replied, "You cannot have *them;* for they work hard, and are tired, they draw the plough; they do their duty, and they ought not to be eaten; but the *hogs* are lazy; they do no work, you may have them to eat, if you wish it." The

Japanese will not even milk their cows, but they allow the calves to have all the milk.

If you wish to know *why* the Japanese will not allow strangers to land, I must relate some events which happened three hundred years ago.

Some Roman Catholic priests from Spain and Portugal settled in the land, and taught the people about Christ, but they taught them also to worship the cross, and the Virgin Mary. Thousands of the Japanese were baptized, and were called Christians. After some years had passed away, the emperor began to fear that the kings of Spain and Portugal would come, and take away his country from him, as they had taken away other countries; so the emperor began to persecute the priests, and all who followed their words. One emperor after another persecuted the Christians. There is a burning mountain in Japan, and down its terrible yawning mouth many Christians were thrown. One emperor commanded his people instead of *worshipping* the cross, to *trample* upon it. To do either —is wicked; to do either is to insult Christ.

All Christians are now hated in Japan. The Dutch tried to persuade the emperors to trust *them;* but they could only get leave to buy and sell at one place, but not to settle in the land.

There are many beautiful things in Japan, especially

boxes, and screens, and cabinets, varnished and ornamented in a curious manner, and these are much admired by great people in Europe. There is silk, too, and tea, and porcelain in Japan; but they are not nearly as fine as China. There is gold also.

There are as many people in Japan, as there are in Britain; for the Japanese are very industrious, and cultivate abundance of rice, and wheat. Oh! how sad to think that so many millions should be living and dying in darkness; for the chief religion is the false, and foolish religion of Buddha, or, as he is called in Japan, "Budso." How many names are given to that deceiver! Buddha in Ceylon; Fo, in China; Gaudama, in Burmah; Codom, in Siam—and Budso in Japan!

What sort of people are the Japanese?

They are a very polite people—much politer than the Chinese, but very proud. They are a learned nation, for they can read and write, and they understand geography, arithmetic, and astronomy. There is a college where many languages are taught, even English. The dress of the gentlemen is elegant;—the loose tunic and trowsers, the sash, and jacket, are made of a kind of fine linen, adorned with various patterns; the stockings are of white jean; sandals are worn upon the feet, but no covering upon the head, although most of the hair is shaven, and the little that remains behind, is tied tightly together; an umbrella or a fan is all that is used to keep off the sun;—except on journeys, and then a large cap of oiled paper, or of plaited grass is worn. The great mark by which a gentleman is known, is wearing two swords.

The Japanese houses are very pretty. In the windows—flower-pots are placed; and when real flowers cannot be had, artificial flowers are used. In great houses, the ladies are shut up in one part; while in the other, company is received. The house is divided into rooms by large screens, and as these can be moved, the rooms can be made larger, or smaller, as the master pleases. There are no chairs, for the Japanese, though so much like the Chinese, do not sit like them on chairs, but on mats beautifully woven. The emperor's palace is called, "The Hall of the Thousand Mats." Every part of a Japanese house is covered with paper, and adorned with paintings, and gold, and silver flowers; even the doors, and the ceilings, are ornamented in this manner. Beautiful boxes, and porcelain jars, add to the beauty of the rooms.

The climate is pleasant, for the winter is short, and the sun is not as hot as in China; so that the ladies, and gentlemen, are almost as fair as Europeans, though the laborers are very dark.

JAPANESE GENTLEMAN. p. 289.

But Japan is exposed to many dangers, from wind, from water, and from fire—three terrible enemies! The waves dash with violence upon the rocky shores; the wind often blows in fearful hurricanes; while earthquakes and hot streams from the burning mountains, fill the people with terror.

But more terrible than any of these—is wickedness; and very wicked customs are observed in Japan. It is very wicked for a man to kill himself, yet in Japan it is the custom for all courtiers who have offended the emperor, to cut open their own bodies with a sword. The little boys of five years old, begin to learn the dreadful art. They do not really cut themselves, but they are shown *how* to do it, that when they are men, they may be able to kill themselves in an elegant manner. How dreadful! Every great man has a white dress, which he never wears, but keeps by him, that he may put it on when he is going to kill himself: and he carries it about with him wherever he goes, for he cannot tell how suddenly he may want it. When a courtier receives a letter sentencing him to die, he invites his friends to a feast; and at the end of it, his sentence is read aloud by the emperor's officer; then he takes his sword, and makes a great gash across his own body; at the same moment, a servant who stands behind him, cuts off his head.

This way of dying is thought very fine, and as a reward, the emperor allows the son of the dead man to occupy his father's place in the court. But *what* a place to have, when at least there may be such a fearful scene! Missionaries cannot come into Japan to teach the people a better way of dying, and to tell them of a happy place after death.

Australia.

THIS is the largest island in the world. It is as large as Europe (which is not an *island*, but a *continent*). But how different is Australia from Europe! Instead of containing, as Europe does, a number of grand kingdoms, it has not one single king. Instead of being filled with people, the greater part of Australia is a desert, or a forest, where a few half naked savages are wandering.

A hundred years ago, there was not a town in the whole island; but now there are a few large towns near the sea-coast, but only a very few. It is the English who built these large towns, and who live in them.

Australia is not so fine a land as Europe, because it has not so many fine rivers; and it is fine *rivers* that make a fine *land*. Most of the rivers in Australia do not deserve the name of rivers; they are more like a number of water-holes, and are often dried up in the summer; but there is one very fine, broad, long, deep river, called the Murray. It flows for twelve hundred miles. Were there several such rivers as the Murray, then Australia would be a fine land indeed.

Why is there so little water? Because there is so little rain. Sometimes for two years together, there are no heavy showers, and the grass withers, and the trees turn brown, and the air is filled with dust. I believe the reason of the want of rain is—that the mountains are not high; for high mountains draw the clouds together. There are no mountains as high as the Alps of Europe; the highest are only half as high.*

The Natives.—The savages of Australia have neither god, nor king. Some heathen countries are full of idols, but there are no idols in the wilds of Australia. No,—like the beasts which perish, these savages live from day to day without prayer, or praise, delighting only in eating and drinking, hunting and dancing.

Most men build some kind of houses; but these savages are satisfied with putting a few boughs together, as a shelter from the storm. There is just room in one of these shelters for a man to creep into it, and lie down to sleep. They do not wish to learn

* The Australian mountains are about seven thousand feet high.

to build better huts, for as they are always running about from place to place, they do not think it worth while to build better.

A native was once sitting in the corner of a white man's hut, and looking as if he enjoyed the warmth. The white men began to laugh at him, for not building a good hut for himself. For some time the black man said nothing, at last he muttered, "Ay, ay, white fellow think it best that-a-way. Black fellow think it best that-a-way." A white man rudely answered, "Then black fellow is a fool." Upon hearing this, the black fellow, quite affronted, got up, and folding his blanket round him, walked out of the hut. How much pride there is in the heart of man! Even a savage thinks a great deal of his own wisdom, and cannot bear to be called a fool.

Sometimes the natives build a house *strong* enough to last during the whole winter, and *large* enough to hold seven or eight people. They make it in the shape of a bee-hive.

Their reason for moving about continually, is that they may get food. They look for it, wherever they go, digging up roots, and grubbing up grubs, and searching the hollows of the trees for *opossums.* (Of these strange animals more shall soon be mentioned.)

The women are the most ill-treated creatures in the

world. The men beat them on their heads whenever they please, and cover them with bruises. A gentleman once saw a poor black woman crying bitterly. When he asked her what was the matter, she told him that her husband was going to beat her for having broken his pipe. The gentleman went to the husband, and entreated him to forgive his "gin" (for that is the name for a *wife* or *woman*). But the man declared he would not forgive her, unless a new pipe was given to him. The gentleman could not promise one to the black man, as there were no pipes to be had in that place. The next morning the poor gin appeared with a broken arm, her cruel husband having beaten her with a thick stick.

The miserable gins are not *beaten* only; they are *half starved*; for their husbands will give them no food, and *they*—poor things—cannot fish or hunt, or shoot; they have nothing but the roots they dig up, and the grubs, and lizards, and snakes they find on the ground. Their looks show how wretchedly they fare; for while the men are often strong and tall, the women are generally thin, and bent, and haggard.

Yet the *woman*, weak as she is, carries all the baggage, not only the babe slung upon her back, but the bag of food, and even her husband's gun and pipe; while the *man* stalks along in his pride, with nothing but his spear in his hand, or at most a light basket upon his arm; for he considers his wife as his beast of burden. At night the woman has to build her own shelter, for the man thinks it quite enough to build one for himself.

Such is the hard lot of a native woman, while she *lives;* and when she *dies,* her body is perched in a tree, as not worth the trouble of burying.

I have already told you, that the natives have no GOD; yet they have a DEVIL, whom they call Yakoo, or debbil-debbil. Of him they are always afraid, for they fancy he goes about devouring children. When any one dies, they say, "Yakoo took him." How different from those happy Christians who can say of their dead, "God took them!"

People who know not God, but only the devil, must be very wicked. These savages show themselves to be children of debbil-debbil by their actions. They kill many of their babes, that they may not have the trouble of nursing them. Old people also they kill, and laugh at the idea of making them "tumble down." One of the most horrible things they do, is making the skulls of their friends into drinking-cups, and they think that by doing so, they show their AFFECTION! They allow the nearest relation to have the skull of the dead person. They will even EAT a little piece of the dead body, just as a mark of love. But generally speaking, it is only their *enemies* they eat, and they *do* eat them whenever they can kill them. There are a great many tribes of natives, and they look upon one another as enemies. If a man of one tribe dare to come, and hunt in the lands of another tribe, he is immediately killed, and his body is eaten.

The bodies of dear friends—are treated with great honor, placed for some weeks on a high platform, and then buried. Mothers prize highly the dead bodies of their children. A traveller met a poor old woman wandering in search of roots, with a stick for digging in her hand, and with no other covering than a little grass mat. On her back she bore a heavy load. What was it? The dead body of her child,—a boy of ten years old; this burden she had borne for three weeks, and she thought she showed her love, by keeping it near her for so long a time. Alas! she knew nothing of the immortal spirit, and how, when washed in Jesus' blood, it is borne by angels into the presence of God.

But though these savages are so wicked, and so wild, they have their amusements. Dancing is the chief amusement. At every full moon, there is a grand dance, called the Corrobory. It is the men who dance, while the women sit by and beat time. Nothing can be more horrible to see than a Corrobory. It is held in the night by the light of blazing fires. The men are made to look more frightful than usual, by great patches, and stripes of red and white clay all over their bodies; and they play all manner of strange antics, and utter all kinds of strange yells; so that you might think it was a dance in HELL, rather than on earth.

It may surprise you to hear these wild creatures have a turn both for music and drawing. There are figures carved upon the rocks, which show their turn for drawing. The figures represent beasts, fishes, and men, and are much better done than could have been supposed. There are few savages who can sing as well as these natives; but the *words* of their songs are very foolish. These are the words of one song,

"Eat great deal, eat, eat, eat;
Eat again, plenty to eat;
Eat more yet, eat, eat, eat."

If a pig could sing, surely this song would just suit its fancy. How sad to think a man who is made to praise God forever and ever, should have no higher joy than eating!

And what is the appearance of these people?

They are ugly, with flat noses, and wide mouths,

but their teeth are white, and their hair is long, glossy, and curly. They adorn their tresses with teeth, and feathers, and dogs' tails; and they rub over their whole body with fish oil and fat. You may imagine, therefore, how unpleasant it must be to come near them.

THE COLONISTS OR SETTLERS.

Once there were only black people in Australia, and no white; *now* there are more white than black; and it is probable, that soon, there will be no black people, but only white. Ever since the white people began to settle there, the black people have been dying away very fast; for the white people have taken away the lands where the blacks used to hunt, and have filled them with their sheep and cattle.

There are two sorts of white people who have come to Australia. They are called "Convicts," and "Colonists."

Convicts are some of the worst of the white people; —thieves, who instead of being kept in prison, were sent to Australia to work hard for many years. It is a sad thing for Australia, that so many thieves have been sent there, because after their punishment was over, and they were set at liberty, some remained in the land, and did a great deal of harm.

Colonists are people who come of their own accord to earn their living as best they can.

It is a common sight when travelling in Australia, to meet a dray drawn by bullocks, laden with furniture, and white people. It is a family going to their new farm. In the dray there are pigs, and you may hear them grunting; there are fowls, too, shut up in a basket; and besides, there are plants and tools. When the family arrive at the place where they mean to settle, they find no house, nor garden, nor fields, only a wild forest. Immediately they pitch a tent for the mother and her daughters to sleep in, while the father, his sons, and his laborers, sleep by the fire in the open air. The next morning, the men begin to fell trees to make a hut, and they finish it in a week;—not a very grand dwelling, it is true, but good enough for the fine weather; the floor is made of the hard clay from the enormous ant hills; the walls—of great slabs of wood; the roof—of wooden tiles, and the windows—of calico. When the hut is finished, a hen-house, and a pig-sty are built, and a dairy also underground. A garden is soon planted, and there the vines, and the peach-trees bear beautiful fruit. The daughters attend to the rearing of the fowls, and the milking of the cows, and soon have a plentiful supply of eggs and butter. The men clear the ground of trees, in order to sow wheat and potatoes. Thus the family soon have all their wants supplied; and they find time by degrees to build a stone house, with eight large rooms; and when it is completed, they give up their wooden hut to one of the laborers. This is the way of life in the "Bush;" for such is the name given to the wild parts of Australia.

Some settlers keep large flocks of sheep, and gain money by selling the wool and the fat, to make cloth and tallow. A shepherd in Australia leads a very lonely life among the hills, and he is obliged to keep ever upon the watch against the wild dogs. These voracious animals prowl about in troops, and cruelly bite numbers of the sheep, and then devour as many as they can. Happily there are no *large* wild beasts, such as wolves, and bears, lions, and tigers; for these would devour the shepherd as well as the sheep.

But there are *men*, called "bush-rangers," as fierce as wild beasts. These are convicts who have escaped from punishment. They often come to the settlers' houses, and murder the inhabitants.

The natives are not nearly as dangerous as these wicked *white* men; indeed *they* are generally very harmless, unless provoked by ill-treatment. They are willing to make themselves useful, by reaping corn, and washing sheep; and a little reward satisfies them, such as a blanket, or an old coat. When some of the flock have strayed, the blacks will take great pains to look for them, and seem as much pleased when they have found them, as if they were their own sheep. The black women can help in the wash-house, and in the farm-yard; but they are too much besmeared with grease to be fit for the kitchen. It is wise never to give a good dinner to a black, till his work is done; because he always eats so much, that he can work no more that day.

Some of these poor blacks are very faithful and affectionate. There was one who lived near a settler's hut, and he used to come there every morning before the master was up; he would enter very gently for fear of waking him,—light the fire by rubbing two pieces of wood together, and set the kettle on to boil; then he would approach the bed, and putting his hand affectionately on the hand of the sleeper, would whisper in his ear, till he saw him open his eyes, when he would greet him with a kind and smiling look. These attentions were the mark of his attachment to the white man.

This black was as faithful, as he was affectionate. Once he was sent by a farmer on a message. It was this, "Take this letter to my brother, and he will give you sixpence, and then spend the sixpence in pipes for me." The black man took the letter, and went towards the place where the brother lived. He met him on horseback. The brother after reading the letter, rode away without giving the sixpence to the bearer. What was the poor black man to do? "Shall I go back," thought he, "without the pipes? No. I will try to get some money." He went to a house that he knew of, and offered to chop some wood for sixpence, and with *that sixpence* he bought the pipes. Was not this being a good servant? This was not eye-service; it was the service of the heart. But there are not many natives like this man. They are generally soon tired of working. For instance, a boy called Jackey, left a good master who would have provided for him, to live again wild in the woods, and went away with the blanket off his bed.

Animals.—There are few of *our* animals in Australia, or of *their* animals in England. There is no hare, no rabbit, no nightingale, no thrush, in Australia. *Once* there were no horses, nor cows, nor sheep, nor pigs; but *now* there are a great many. Much terrified were the natives at the sight of the first horse which came from England; for they had never seen such a large animal before.

The largest beast in Australia is the Kangaroo, remarkable for its short fore-legs, and its great strong hind-legs, and for the pocket in which it shelters its little one. It is a gentle creature, and can be easily tamed. A pet kangaroo may often be seen walking about a settler's garden, cropping the grass upon the lawn. But though easily *tamed*, a wild kangaroo is not easily *caught*; for it makes immense springs in the air, far higher than a horse could leap, though it is not as big as a sheep. When hunted by dogs, it gets, when it can, into the water, and turning round, and standing still, dips the dogs, one by one, till it drowns them.

There is another beast, called the opossum, not much bigger than a large cat, and it also has a pocket for its young ones. But instead of cropping the grass, it eats the leaves of trees. It has a gentle face like a deer, and a long tail like a monkey. It hides itself, as the squirrel does, in the hollows of trees. Like the owl, it is never seen in the day, but at night it comes out to feed. The blacks are very cunning in finding out the holes where the opossums are hidden, and they know how to drag them out by their long tails, without getting bitten by their sharp teeth. With the skin of the opossum the natives make a cloak.

The wild dogs, or dingoes, are odious animals. They may be heard yelling at night to the terror of the shepherd, and the farmer. They are bold enough to rush into a yard, and to carry off a calf, or a pig; and when they have dragged it into the woods, they cruelly eat the legs first, and do not kill it for a long while.

These three—the kangaroo, the opossum, and the dingo,—are the principal beasts of Australia.

Among the birds, the emu is the most remarkable. It is nearly as tall as an ostrich, and has beautiful soft feathers, though not as beautiful as the ostrich's. But the most curious point in the emu is,—it has no tongue. You may suppose, therefore, that it is neither a singing bird, nor a talking bird; it only makes a little noise in its throat. But if *it* is silent, there are numbers of parrots, and cockatoos, to fill the air with their screams. In England, these birds are thought a great deal of, but in Australia, they are killed to make into pies, or into soup. Parrot-pie and cockatoo-soup, are common dishes there. However, many of the parrots and cockatoos, are caught by the blacks, and sold to the English, who send them to England in the ships.

There are not such singing birds in Australia, as there are here. Though there is a robin red-breast there, he does not sing as sweetly as he does here. But there are *laughing* birds in Australia. There is a bird called the "laughing jackass." He laughs very loud three times a day. He begins in the morning ;—suddenly a hoarse loud laugh is heard,—then another, then another,—till a whole troop of birds seem laughing all together, and go on laughing for a few minutes ;—and then they are all quiet again. Such a noise must awaken many a sleeper on his bed. At noon the laugh is heard again. At evening there is another general fit of laughter. These birds are not like children, who laugh at no particular hour, but often twenty times a day. The laughing jackass is almost as useful as a clock, and it is called, "the bushman's clock."

BOTANY BAY.

This is a famous place, for here the English first settled, and here it was thieves were sent from England as a punishment. Some were sent there for fourteen years, and some for twenty-one years, and some for life. How did the place get the beautiful name of Botany? which means "the knowledge of flowers." Because there were so many beautiful flowers seen there, when Captain Cook first beheld it.

Yet the name Botany Bay, does not seem beautiful to us; for it reminds us not of roses, but of rogues; not of violets, but of violent men; not of lilies, but of villains.

SYDNEY.

This town is close to Botany Bay. It is the largest town in Australia. It is a very wicked city, because so many convicts have been sent there. Many of the people are the children of convicts, and have been brought up very ill by their parents. Of course there are many robberies in such a city, far more than there are in London. Who would like to live there! yet it is a fine city, and by the sea-side, with a harbor, where hundreds of ships might ride,—safe from the storm. It is plain, too, that Sydney is full of rich people, for the streets are thronged with carriages, driving rapidly along. The convicts often become rich, after their time of punishment is over, by keeping public-houses, and when rich they keep carriages.

If you were in Sydney, you would hardly think you were in a savage island; for you would see no savages in the streets. What is become of those who once lived in these parts? They are all dead, or gone to other parts of the island. The last black near Sydney, used to talk of the old times, and say, "When I was a pick-a-ninny, plenty of black fellow then. Only one left now, mitter."

ADELAIDE.

It is much better to live here than in Sydney, because convicts have never been sent here. Numbers of honest poor people are leaving England and Ireland, every year, to go to Adelaide. When they arrive at the coast, they get into cars, and are driven seven miles, passing by many pretty cottages, and gardens, till they arrive at Adelaide. There they find themselves in the midst of gardens; for the houses are not crowded together, as in our English towns, but are placed in the midst of trees, and flowers, and grass; because there is plenty of room in Australia.

But there is one great evil both in Sydney and in Adelaide, which is the dust blown from the desert, and which almost chokes the inhabitants. If there were more rain in Australia, there would be less dust.

Australia is divided into three parts:—

I. New South Wales. Capital, Sydney.

II. Western Australia. Capital, Perth.

III. South Australia. Capital, Adelaide.

Van Dieman's Land.

THIS island is as cool as Great Britain; yet 't is not a pleasant land to live in; for it is filled with convicts. There are no natives there now; they died away gradually, except a few, who were taken by the English to a small island near, called "Flinder's Island." They were taken there that they might be safe; yet they never ceased to sigh, and to cry after their native land.

THE YOUNG SAVAGES.

Many travellers have tried to see the land in the midst of Australia, but hitherto they have not succeeded. After going a little way, they have been obliged to return, and why? Because they have found no water.

I will give you an account of the journey of Mr. Eyre. This traveller wished to go into the midst of the land, but finding he could not, he travelled along the coast, at that part called the Great Bight (or the Great Bay).

He set out from Adelaide with a large party, but various accidents occurred by the way, and at last he found himself with only one Englishman, and three native boys. The eldest was almost a man. His name was Wylie, and he was a good-tempered, lively youth. The second was named Neramberein. I shall have nothing good to relate of him, but a great deal of evil; for he was indeed a very wicked boy. The youngest was called Cootachah—a boy who was easily induced to follow bad examples.

Mr. Eyre was the chief person in the party, and his English companion was Mr. Baxter. Ten horses carried the packages, and six sheep were made to follow, that they might be killed one by one for food.

All these poor animals suffered terribly from want of water. Sometimes they went a hundred miles without a refreshing draught. The horses became so weak, that the travellers were unwilling to mount their backs; and as for the sheep, they could scarcely crawl along.

Many ways of getting water were tried. One way was digging up the roots of trees. A little,—a very little,—water may often be squeezed out of the end of a root; because the root is the mouth of the tree, and sucks up water from the ground. Another way of getting water was by gathering up the dew in a sponge. Enough dew to make a cup of tea might sometimes be obtained; but not enough for the poor beasts to have any. When the travellers, by digging, could make a well, then they were glad indeed; for then the beasts could be refreshed as well as themselves.

The whole party were become so weak from fatigue and thirst, that they could not get on fast, and they found it necessary to save their food as much as possible, that it might last to the end of the long journey. They took a little flour every day out of their bag, and made it into a paste. Sometimes they caught a fish, or shot a bird or beast, and then they had a hearty meal. When they killed one of their sheep, then they had plenty of mutton. At last, all the sheep were killed but one.

It happened at this time, that one of the horses was so sick that he could not move. It was plain he would soon die; therefore the travellers determined to kill him, and eat his flesh. Mr. Eyre was grieved at the thought of killing his horse, neither could he bear the idea of eating horse flesh; but then he feared, that if the horse were not killed, the whole party would be starved.

The native boys were delighted when they knew the horse was to be eaten; for they had long been fretting for more food. They would like to have devoured it *all* on the spot; but they were not allowed to do so; the greater part of the flesh was cut off in thin slices, dipped in salt water, and then hung up in the sun to dry, to serve as provision for many days to come. The boys were permitted to devour the rest of the carcase.

With what haste they prepared the feast! They made a fire close to the carcase, and then cut off lumps of flesh, which they roasted quickly, and then ate. They spent the whole afternoon in this manner, looking more like ravenous wolves than human creatures. When night came, they were not willing to leave their meat, but took as much as ever they could carry into their beds, that they might eat whenever they awoke. Next day, they returned to the roasting and eating, and the next night again they took meat with them to bed.

Mr. Eyre wondered at their gluttony, and he thought it necessary to give them an allowance of food, instead of letting them eat as much as they liked. He gave five pounds of meat to each boy every day. Five pounds is as much as a shoulder of mutton—and ten English boys would think it quite enough for dinner; but the Australian boys were not satisfied.

Mr. Eyre began to suspect that in the night they stole some of the meat hanging up to dry on the trees. Therefore one night he weighed the meat, and in the morning weighed it again. He found that four pounds were gone. He thought it was very ungrateful of boys, to whom he gave so much, to steal from his small stock. As a punishment he gave them less meat next day than usual.

He entreated the boys to tell him who was the thief. The eldest and youngest declared that they had not stolen any meat; but Neramberein would not answer at all, and looked sulky and angry, and muttered something about going away, and taking Wylie with him. Mr. Eyre replied, that he might go if he pleased, while at the same time he warned him of the dangers of the way.

The next morning, as soon as breakfast was over, the three boys all rose up and walked away. Mr. Eyre called back the youngest, as he felt he was misled by his elders; but he let the others go. They had stayed with him till the horse was all eaten up, except the dried pieces—but now they hoped to get more food, when travelling alone, than with Mr. Eyre.

As soon as the boys were gone, Mr. Eyre determined to stop some time longer where he was, that he might not overtake them. There was one sheep still remaining, and which seemed very restless all by itself. This sheep was killed for food, and in that place there was plenty of water; so that the little company fared well that day and the next; especially as Mr. Baxter had the good fortune to kill an eagle, which made an excellent stew.

Just as the travellers had finished their evening meal, they were astonished to see the two runaway boys approaching. Wylie came running up, declaring that both he and his companions were sorry for their bad behavior, and were anxious to be received again, not being able to get enough to eat. But though Wylie acted in this frank manner, his companion was very sulky. He said nothing, but seated himself by the fire, pouting and frowning, and evidently much vexed at being obliged to come back. Mr. Eyre thought it well to give the boys a lecture on their bad conduct, especially upon their thefts; for they now owned that they had stolen meat from the trees, though they had before denied it. But though Mr. Eyre reproved the boys, he treated them very kindly, for he gave them some tea, and bread and meat for supper.

The next day the whole party continued their journey. They were obliged to be very sparing of their food, lest when it was gone they should get no more. But their greatest trial was the want of water.

After travelling during four days, they stopped one evening in a rocky place at the top of high cliffs, hoping that if any rain should fall, some might be caught in the hollow places among the rocks. That evening they ate no supper; for having had dinner, they might do without supper.

Before they lay down to sleep, they made themselves places to sleep in, by setting up boughs, as shelters from the wind. They also piled up their goods in a great heap, and covered it with oil skin, to keep out the damp. Mr. Eyre did not sleep when the rest did, for he undertook to watch the horses till eleven at night, and then he agreed to change places with Mr. Baxter.

The hour was almost come, and Mr. Eyre was beginning to lead the horses towards the sleeping place, when he was startled by hearing a gun go off. He called out,—but receiving no answer, he grew alarmed, and leaving the horses, ran towards the spot, whence the noise had come.

Presently he met Wylie, running very fast, and crying out, "Oh! Massa, Oh! Massa, come here."

"What is the matter?" inquired Mr. Eyre.

Wylie made no answer.

With hurried steps, Mr. Eyre accompanied him towards the camp. What a sight struck his eyes! His friend Baxter, lying on the ground, weltering in his blood, and in the agonies of DEATH.

The two younger boys were not there, and the goods which had been covered by the oil-skin, lay scattered in confusion on the ground. It was too clear that one of the boys had KILLED poor Baxter. No doubt it was Neramberein who had done it!

It seems that the boys had attempted to steal some of the goods, and that while they were gathering them together, Baxter had awaked, and had come forth from his sleeping place, and that *then* one of the boys had shot him.

Mr. Eyre raised the dying man from the ground where he was lying prostrate, and he then found that a ball had entered his left breast, and that his life was fast departing. In a few minutes he expired!

What were the feelings of the lonely traveller! Here he was in the midst of a desert, with no companion but one young savage, and that young savage was not one whom he could trust; for he knew not what part Wylie had taken in the deeds of the night. He suspected that he had intended to go away with the other boys, but that when Baxter was murdered, he had grown alarmed. Wylie indeed denied that he had known anything of the robbery, but then he was not a boy whose word could be believed.

The remainder of that dreadful night was passed by Mr. Eyre, in watching the horses. Anxiously he waited for the first streak of daylight. He then drove the horses to the camp, and once more beheld the body of his fellow-traveller. How suddenly had his soul been hurried into eternity, and into the presence of his God!

It was Wylie's business to light the fire, and prepare the breakfast. Meanwhile, Mr. Eyre examined the baggage to see how much had been stolen. These were the chief articles he missed. All the bread, consisting of five loaves, some mutton, tea and sugar, tobacco and pipes, a small keg of water, and two guns. And what was left for the traveller? A large quantity of flour, a large keg of water, some tea and sugar, a gun, and pistols. But would these have been left, had the ungrateful boys been strong enough to carry them away?

Mr. Eyre desired before leaving the fatal spot to bury the body of his friend; but the rocks around were so hard, that it was impossible to dig a grave. All he was able to do, was to wrap the corpse in a blanket before he abandoned it forever.

Slowly and silently he left the sorrowful spot, leading one horse, while Wylie drove the others after it. During the heat of the day, they stopped to rest. It was four in the afternoon, and they were soon going to set out again, when they perceived at a distance—TWO WHITE FIGURES! two white figures! and soon knew them to be the two guilty boys, wrapped in their blankets.

Mr. Eyre had some fear lest the young murderer should shoot him also; yet he thought it wise to advance boldly towards him, with his gun in his hand. He perceived that each of the wicked youths held a gun, and seemed ready to shoot. But as he approached, they drew back. He wished to speak to them in order to persuade them not to follow him on his journey, but to go another way; however he could not get near them; but he heard them cry out, "O Massa, we don't want you; we want Wylie." The boys repeated the name of Wylie over and over again; yet Wylie answered not, but remained quietly with the horses. At length Mr. Eyre turned away, and continued his journey. The boys followed at some distance, calling out for Wylie till the darkness came on.

Mr. Eyre was so anxious to get beyond the reach of these wicked youths, that he walked eighteen miles that evening. And he never saw them again! I do not know whether he had ever told them of the true

God, of that EYE which never SLEEPS, of that EYE which beholds ROBBERS and MURDERERS in the night; —but whether he had told them or not of this great God, they must have KNOWN that they were acting wickedly when they robbed their benefactor, and murdered his friend; and they must have felt very MISERABLE after they had done those deeds.

Alone with Wylie, Mr. Eyre pursued his journey along the high cliffs of the Great Bight, or Bay.

For five days they were without water for the horses; at last they dug some wells in the sand. But by this time one of the horses was grown so weak, that he could scarcely crawl along. This horse, Mr. Eyre determined to kill for food. Wylie, delighted with the idea, exclaimed, "Massa, I shall sit up, and eat the whole night." And he kept his word. While his master was skinning the poor beast, he made a fire close by, and soon began tearing off bits of flesh, roasting, and eating them, as fast as he could. Mr. Eyre, after cutting off the best parts of the flesh to dry, allowed Wylie to eat the rest. See the young glutton, with the head, the feet, and the inside, permitted to devour it as best he could! He hastened to make an oven, in which to bake about twenty pounds to feast upon during the night. It is not wonderful, if during that night he was heard to make a dismal groaning, and to complain that he was very ill. He *said*, indeed, that it was *working* too *hard*, had made him ill, but his master thought it was *eating* too *much*, for whenever he woke, he found the boy gnawing a bone.

Next day, Wylie was not able to spend his whole time over the carcase, for he had to go, and look for a lost foal; but the day after, it was hard to get him away from the bones.

For some time the travellers lived upon dried horse flesh, with a kangaroo, or a fish, as a little change. Wylie continued to eat immoderately, though often rolling upon the ground, and crying out, "Mendyat," or ill.

One night he appeared to be in a very ill-humor, and Mr. Eyre tried to find out the reason. At last Wylie said in an angry tone, "The dogs have eaten the skin." It seems he had hung the skin of a kangaroo upon a bush, intending to eat it by-and-bye, and the wild dogs had stolen the dainty morsel. Wylie was restored to his usual good-humor by the sight of some fine fishes his master had caught. Next time the boy shot a kangaroo, he took good care of the skin, folding it up, and hiding it.

One day he was so happy as to catch two opossums in a tree. His master determined to see how Wylie would behave, if left entirely to himself. He sat silently by the fire, while Wylie was cooking one opossum. The boy, having got it ready for his supper, took the other to his sleeping place. His master inquired what he intended to do with it. Wylie replied, "I shall be hungry in the morning, and I am keeping it for my breakfast." Then Mr. Eyre perceived that the greedy boy intended to offer him neither supper nor breakfast. Accordingly he took out his bag of flour, and said to Wylie, "Very well, we will each eat our own food; you eat the opossums you shot, and I eat the flour I have; and I will give you no more." In this manner, Mr. Eyre hoped to show the boy the folly of his selfishness. Wylie was frightened at the idea of getting no more flour, and immediately offered the smaller opossum to his master, and promised to cook it himself. What a selfish, and ungrateful boy! Wylie had a wicked heart by nature, and so have *we*. Only *he* had not been taught what was right, as *we* have been. This is a prayer which would suit well every child, and every man in the world, "Create in me a clean heart, O God, and renew a right spirit within me."

Mr. Eyre continued to be kind to Wylie, though he saw the boy did not really love him.

But the troubles of the journey were nearly at an

end. At last the travellers saw a ship a few miles from the shore. Oh! how anxious they were that the sailors should see them! What could they do! They kindled a fire on a rock, and they made a great deal of smoke come out of the fire. Soon a boat was seen approaching the shore. How great was the joy of the weary travellers. The sailors in the boat were Frenchmen, but they were not the less kind on that account. They invited Mr. Eyre and Wylie to accompany them to their ship.

When the young savage found himself on board, he was almost wild with delight, for he had now as much to eat as he could desire, and he began eating biscuits so fast, that the sailors began to be afraid lest he should eat them all; and they were glad to give him fishes instead, as they could catch plenty of them.

For twelve days Wylie and his master lived in the ship, and then left it, laden with provisions, and dressed in warm clothes.

They had still many miles to go along the shore, but they suffered no more from want of food and water.

Great was their rapture when they first caught sight of the hills of St. George's Sound; for then they knew their journey would soon end. But they had rivers to cross on the way, and in trying to get the norses over, they nearly lost the poor beasts, and their own lives too. For three days their clothes were dripping with wet, and the last night was one of the worst; but then they knew it was the LAST, and that thought enabled them to bear all. So does the Christian feel when near the end of his journey. He is in the midst of storms, and wading through deep waters, even the deep waters of DEATH; but he knows that he is near HOME.

It was in the midst of a furious storm, that these travellers arrived at their journey's end. Though they were now close to the town of Albany, neither man nor beast were to be seen; for neither would venture out. At last, a native appeared, and he knew Wylie, and greeted him joyfully, telling him at the same time that his friends had given him up for dead a long while ago. This native, by a loud shrill cry, let his countrymen know that Wylie was found; and presently a multitude of men, women, and children, came rushing rapidly from the town, and up the hill to meet him. His parents and brethren folded him in their arms, while all around welcomed him with shouts of joy. His master was kindly received at the house of a friend; but he did not meet with so warm a welcome as Wylie, for he was not like him in the midst of his family.

The kind master overlooked all Wylie's faults during the journey, and remembered only his kindness in keeping with him to the end. He even spoke in his favor to the government, requesting that Wylie might have a daily allowance of food as a reward for his good conduct. What great reason had this young savage to rejoice that he had not listened to the enticements of his wicked comrades, when they called him so often by his name, and tried to induce him to forsake his kind master!

LITTLE MICKEY.

Mickey was born in the wilds of Australia; yet he was a highly favored boy; for he became servant to a missionary. This was far better than being, like Wylie, the companion of a traveller.

Mickey was a merry and active little fellow, and was a great favorite with his master's children. The older ones taught him to read, and the little ones played with him. During the day, Mickey took care of the cattle, and at night he slept in a shed close by his master's house. He might have been a happy boy, but he soon fell into sin and sorrow.

One evening he was in the cooking-house, eating

his supper with another native boy, his fellow-servant. The oven was hot, and the bread was baking. Mickey opened the door of the oven, and looked in. That was wrong; it was the first step towards evil. Mickey had eaten a good supper, and ought to have been satisfied; but, like his countrymen, he had an enormous appetite, and was always ready to eat too much when he could. He took some of the hot bread, and gave some to his fellow-servant. How like was his conduct to that of Eve, when she took the fruit, and gave some to Adam!

That night Mickey was nowhere to be found, nor his little fellow-servant either. Where could they be? Their master sent people to search for them; but no one had seen them. It seemed strange indeed, that a boy who had been so kindly treated, and who had seemed as happy as Mickey, should run away. The good missionary and his children were in great grief, fearing that some accident had befallen the lads.

But when the time came to take the bread out of the oven, they began to suspect why Mickey had gone away. They saw some one had stolen large pieces of bread. They said, "Perhaps it was Mickey who stole the bread, and perhaps he is ashamed, and so he has run away." What a pity it was that Mickey did not come, and confess his fault; he would have been pardoned and restored to favor. Even a good boy may fall into a great sin; but then he will own it, and ask forgiveness, both of God and man. Still Mickey was not like those hardened boys who robbed Mr. Eyre, for he was ashamed.

Month after month passed away, but no Mickey appeared. The missionary feared that the boy would never return, but live and die amongst his heathen countrymen.

One day, however, he was told that a man was at the door, who wanted to speak to him.

"Who is he?" inquired the missionary.

"A schoolmaster, sir," replied the servant.

"And what does he want?"

"He has brought with him some native boys, and he wants you to come out and see them, and speak a few words to them about their Saviour."

The missionary gladly consented to go out to behold so pleasing a sight, as a school of native boys. As soon as he appeared, several young voices called out, "Mickey no come."

The missionary was surprised, and inquired of the boys, "What do you mean? where is Mickey?"

"Mickey no come," repeated the boys. "He too much frightened."

"Why is he afraid?" asked the missionary.

"Because he steal de bread," replied the boys.

The missionary now began to look around, and soon espied Mickey, trying to hide himself behind a fence. He called him; but Mickey, instead of coming, went further off. Two or three boys then ran towards him, and attempted to bring him back, but Mickey resisted.

The missionary then went into the house hoping that the trembling culprit, seeing he was gone, would come out of his hiding-place.

Very soon he was told, that Mickey was standing with the other boys at the door. Then the good missionary appeared again. Looking kindly at Mickey, he said, "Why did you run rway?"

"Because me steal de bread; me very sorry."

The missionary held out his hand to the sorrowful offender, saying, "I forgive you, Mickey." The boy eagerly seized the kind hand, and holding it fast, and looking earnestly up in the missionary's face, he said, "When me steal again, you must whip me—and whip me—and whip me—very—very much." Again the missionary assured the boy he had entirely forgiven him—and then Mickey began to jump about for joy.

How glad Mickey would have been to return to the service of his old master! But that could not be; for that master was just going to set sail for England, to visit his home and friends, and he could not take Mickey with him. Just before he went, he provided a feast for many of the native children, and gave them a parting address. Mickey was there—no longer afraid—but glad to look up in the face of his beloved friend; for now he knew he was forgiven.

When the moment came to say "Farewell," the children ran forward, eager to grasp the missionary's hand—but none pressed that hand so warmly and so sorrowfully, as the little runaway.

I know not whether that generous master, and that penitent servant ever again met upon earth; but I have much hope they will meet in heaven; for Mickey seems to have been sorry for his sin; and we know the promise: "If we confess our sins, God is faithful and just to forgive us our sins." And why? Because the blood of Christ cleanseth from all sin. There are many sinners who were once as much afraid of God, as Mickey was of his master; but who have been pardoned, and who will be present at his HEAVENLY FEAST.

THE END.